Working Papers Chapters 1-17

Accounting, 23e or Financial Accounting, 11e

Carl S. Warren
Professor Emeritus of Accounting
University of Georgia, Athens

James M. Reeve
Professor Emeritus of Accounting
University of Tennessee, Knoxville

Jonathan E. Duchac
Professor of Accounting
Wake Forest University

SOUTH-WESTERN
CENGAGE Learning™

Australia • Brazil • Japan • Korea • Mexico • Singapore • Spain • United Kingdom • United States

SOUTH-WESTERN
CENGAGE Learning

For product information and technology assistance, contact us at **Cengage Learning Academic Resource Center, 1-800-423-0563**

For permission to use material from this text or product, submit all requests online at **www.cengage.com/permissions**
Further permissions questions can be emailed to **permissionrequest@cengage.com**

ISBN-13: 978-0-324-66398-3
ISBN-10: 0-324-66398-6

South-Western, Cengage Learning
2640 Eagan Woods Drive
Suite 220
Eagan, MN 55121

Cengage Learning is a leading provider of customized learning solutions with office locations around the globe, including Singapore, the United Kingdom, Australia, Mexico, Brazil, and Japan. Locate your local office at: **international.cengage.com/region**

Cengage Learning products are represented in Canada by Nelson Education, Ltd.

For your course and learning solutions, visit **academic.cengage.com**

Purchase any of our products at your local college store or at our preferred online store **www.ichapters.com**

Printed in the United States of America
2 3 4 5 6 7 11 10 09 08

CONTENTS

PREFACE

The working papers include problem-specific forms for preparing solutions for Exercises, A&B Problems, the Continuing Problem, and the Comprehensive Problems from the textbook. These forms, with preprinted headings, provide a structure for the problems, which will help you get started and save you time.

Based on students' testimonials and instructors' feedback, the forms in the working papers have been streamlined to make them simpler to use and to better reflect the changing environment of business. For example, the vertical rules that separated digits of numbers entered into journals, ledgers, and statements have been removed, making it easier to write in numbers. Also, the format of the end-of-period spreadsheet (work sheet) has been updated to better resemble an actual electronic spreadsheet.

Note that when entering whole amounts into the forms, your instructor will direct you on whether to include a decimal point and zeroes (e.g., 100.00) or to omit those (e.g., 100).

Name ______________________

EXERCISE 1-1

1. ________ 6. ________ 11. ________
2. ________ 7. ________ 12. ________
3. ________ 8. ________ 13. ________
4. ________ 9. ________ 14. ________
5. ________ 10. ________ 15. ________

EXERCISE 1-2

EXERCISE 1-3

1. ________ 6. ________
2. ________ 7. ________
3. ________ 8. ________
4. ________ 9. ________
5. ________ 10. ________

EXERCISE 1-4

EXERCISE 1-5

EXERCISE 1-6

	Assets	=	Liabilities	+	Owner's Equity
a.	________	=	$250,000	+	$780,000
b.	$125,000	=	________	+	39,500
c.	60,000	=	7,500	+	________

EXERCISE 1-7

a. ______________________

b. ______________________

c. ______________________

d. ______________________

e. ______________________

EXERCISE 1-8

a. Accounts payable: ______________________

b. Cash: ______________________

c. Fees earned: ______________________

d. Land: ______________________

e. Supplies: ______________________

f. Wages expense: ______________________

EXERCISE 1-9

a. ______________________

b. ______________________

c. ______________________

d. ______________________

e. ______________________

EXERCISE 1-10

a. **(1)** Assets: ______________________

(2) Liabilities: ______________________

(3) Owner's equity: ______________________

b. **(1)** Assets: ______________________

(2) Liabilities: ______________________

(3) Owner's equity: ______________________

EXERCISE 1-11

1. Expenses: ______________________

2. Revenues: ______________________

3. Owner's investments: ______________________

4. Owner's withdrawals: ______________________

Name ______________________________

EXERCISE 1-12

1. ______________________
2. ______________________
3. ______________________
4. ______________________
5. ______________________
6. ______________________
7. ______________________
8. ______________________
9. ______________________
10. ______________________

EXERCISE 1-13

a. (1) ______________________

(2) ______________________

(3) ______________________

(4) ______________________

(5) ______________________

(6) ______________________

(7) ______________________

b. ______________________

c. ______________________

d. ______________________

e. ______________________

EXERCISE 1-14

____

____

____

____

____

____

____

EXERCISE 1-15

Jupiter:

Mercury:

Saturn:

Venus:

EXERCISE 1-16

1. Accounts Payable: ______________________________
2. Cash: ______________________________
3. Fees Earned: ______________________________
4. Land: ______________________________
5. Sarah Neil, Capital: ______________________________
6. Supplies: ______________________________
7. Supplies Expense: ______________________________
8. Utilities Expense: ______________________________
9. Wages Expense: ______________________________
10. Wages Payable: ______________________________

EXERCISE 1-17

1. Accounts Payable: ______________________________
2. Cash: ______________________________
3. Fees Earned: ______________________________
4. Land: ______________________________
5. Sarah Neil, Capital: ______________________________
6. Supplies: ______________________________
7. Supplies Expense: ______________________________
8. Utilities Expense: ______________________________
9. Wages Expense: ______________________________
10. Wages Payable: ______________________________

EXERCISE 1-18

Statement of Owner's Equity

EXERCISE 1-19

Income Statement

Name ____________________

EXERCISE 1-20

Earth:

Mars:

Neptune:

Pluto:

EXERCISE 1-21

a.

Balance Sheet

Balance Sheet

b.	
c.	

Name ______________________________

EXERCISE 1-22

a. Accounts payable: ______________________________
b. Cash equivalents: ______________________________
c. Crude oil inventory: ______________________________
d. Equipment: ______________________________
e. Exploration expenses: ______________________________
f. Income taxes payable: ______________________________
g. Investments: ______________________________
h. Long-term debt: ______________________________
i. Marketable securities: ______________________________
j. Notes and loans payable: ______________________________
k. Notes receivable: ______________________________
l. Operating expenses: ______________________________
m. Prepaid taxes: ______________________________
n. Sales: ______________________________
o. Selling expenses: ______________________________

EXERCISE 1-23

1. Cash received as owner's investment: ______________________________
2. Cash paid for land: ______________________________
3. Cash received from fees earned: ______________________________
4. Cash paid for expenses: ______________________________

EXERCISE 1-24

Statement of Cash Flows

Name ______________________________

EXERCISE 1-25

EXERCISE 1-25, Continued

(optional)

Income Statement

Statement of Owner's Equity

EXERCISE 1-25, Concluded

(optional)

Balance Sheet

EXERCISE 1-26

a.

b.

c.

EXERCISE 1-27

a.

b.

c.

d.

Name ____________________

PROBLEM 1-1 ___

1.

	Assets			= Liabilities +	Owner's Equity								
	Cash +	Accounts Receivable +	Supplies =	Accounts Payable +	Capital −	Drawing +	Fees Earned −	Rent Exp. −	Sal. Exp. −	Supp. Exp. −	Auto Exp. −	Misc. Exp.
a.												
b.												
Bal.												
c.												
Bal.												
d.												
Bal.												
e.												
Bal.												
f.												
Bal.												
g.												
Bal.												
h.												
Bal.												
i.												
Bal.												
j.												
Bal.												

2.

Name ______________________________

PROBLEM 1-2 ___

1.

Income Statement

2.

Statement of Owner's Equity

PROBLEM 1-2 ___, Concluded

3.

Balance Sheet

Name ____________________________

PROBLEM 1-3 ___

1.

Income Statement

2.

Statement of Owner's Equity

PROBLEM 1-3 ___, Concluded

3.

Balance Sheet

4. (Optional)

Statement of Cash Flows

Name ____________________

PROBLEM 1-4 ___

1.

	Assets			=	Liabilities	+	Owner's Equity															
	Cash	+	Supplies	=	Accounts Payable	+	Capital	–	Drawing	+	Sales Comm.	–	Office Sal. Exp.	–	Rent Exp.	–	Auto Exp.	–	Supp. Exp.	–	Misc. Exp.
a.																					
b.																					
Bal.																					
c.																					
Bal.																					
d.																					
Bal.																					
e.																					
Bal.																					
f.																					
Bal.																					
g.																					
Bal.																					
h.																					
Bal.																					
i.																					
Bal.																					

PROBLEM 1-4 ___, Continued

2.

Income Statement

Statement of Owner's Equity

PROBLEM 1-4 ___, Concluded

Balance Sheet

Name ______________________________

PROBLEM 1-5 ___

1.

Assets							=	Liabilities	+	Owner's Equity
Cash	+	Accounts Receivable	+	Supplies	+	Land	=	Accounts Payable	+	____________, Capital
________	+	________	+	________	+	________	=	________	+	________, Capital
		______________________					=	________	+	________, Capital
		______________________					=		+	________, Capital

Name ____________________

PROBLEM 1-5 ___, Continued

2.

	Assets				= Liabilities +	Owner's Equity									
	Cash +	Accts. Rec. +	Supplies +	Land =	Accts. Pay. +	____ Capital –	____ Drawing +	Dry Cleaning Revenue –	Dry Cleaning Exp. –	Wages Exp. –	Rent Exp. –	Supp. Exp. –	Truck Exp. –	Util. Exp. –	Misc. Exp.
a.															
b.															
c.															
d.															
e.															
f.															
g.															
h.															
i.															
j.															
k.															
l.															

PROBLEM 1-5 ___, Continued

3a.

Income Statement

3b.

Statement of Owner's Equity

PROBLEM 1-5 ___, Continued

3c.

Balance Sheet

PROBLEM 1-5 ___, Concluded

4. (Optional)

Statement of Cash Flows

Name ________________________________

PROBLEM 1-6 ___

a. ________________________________

b. ________________________________

c. ________________________________

d. ________________________________

e. ________________________________

f. ________________________________

g. ________________________________

h. ________________________________

i. ________________________________

j. ________________________________

k. ________________________________

l. ________________________________

m. ________________________________

n. ________________________________

o. ________________________________

p. ________________________________

q. ________________________________

Name ______________________

CONTINUING PROBLEM

1.

	ASSETS			= LIABILITIES +	OWNER'S EQUITY											
	Cash	+ Accts. Rec.	+ Supplies	= Accts. Pay.	+ Lee Chang, Capital	– Lee Chang, Drawing	+ Fees Earned	– Music Exp.	– Office Rent Exp.	– Equip. Rent Exp.	– Adv. Exp.	– Wages Exp.	– Util. Exp.	– Sup. Exp.	– Misc. Exp.
6/1															
6/2															
Bal.															
6/2															
Bal.															
6/4															
Bal.															
6/6															
Bal.															
6/8															
Bal.															
6/12															
Bal.															
6/13															
Bal.															
6/16															
Bal.															
6/22															
Bal.															
6/25															
Bal.															
6/29															
Bal.															
6/30															
Bal.															

Name ____________________

CONTINUING PROBLEM, Continued

1.

	ASSETS			= LIABILITIES +	OWNER'S EQUITY										
	Cash	+ Accts. Rec.	+ Supplies	= Accts. Pay.	+ Lee Chang, Capital	– Lee Chang, Drawing	+ Fees Earned	– Music Exp.	– Office Rent Exp.	– Equip. Rent Exp.	– Adv. Exp.	– Wages Exp.	– Util. Exp.	– Sup. Exp.	– Misc. Exp.
Bal.															
6/30															
Bal.															
6/30															
Bal.															
6/30															
Bal.															
6/30															
Bal.															
6/30															
Bal.															
6/30															
Bal.															

CONTINUING PROBLEM, Continued

2.

Income Statement

3.

Statement of Owner's Equity

CONTINUING PROBLEM, Concluded

4.

Balance Sheet

Name ______________________________

EXERCISE 2-1

Accounts Payable: ______________________________

Air Traffic Liability: ______________________________

Aircraft Fuel Expense: ______________________________

Cargo and Mail Revenue: ______________________________

Commissions: ______________________________

Flight Equipment: ______________________________

Landing Fees: ______________________________

Passenger Revenue: ______________________________

Purchase Deposits for Flight Equipment: ______________________________

Spare Parts and Supplies: ______________________________

EXERCISE 2-2

Account	Account Number
Accounts Payable.................	________
Accounts Receivable............	________
Cash	________
Fees Earned	________
Land.....................................	________
Miscellaneous Expense	________
Supplies Expense.................	________
Tony Newbaurer, Capital	________
Tony Newbaurer, Drawing	________
Wages Expense	________

EXERCISE 2-3

Balance Sheet Accounts

Acct #	Account Name
	1. Assets
	2. Liabilities
	3. Owner's Equity

Income Statement Accounts

Acct #	Account Name
	4. Revenue
	5. Expenses

EXERCISE 2-4

a. and b.

Transaction	Account Debited: Type	Account Debited: Effect	Account Credited: Type	Account Credited: Effect
(1)	asset	+	owner's equity	+
(2)				
(3)				
(4)				
(5)				
(6)				
(7)				
(8)				
(9)				

EXERCISE 2-5

JOURNAL PAGE

	DATE		DESCRIPTION	POST. REF.	DEBIT	CREDIT	
1							1
2							2
3							3
4							4
5							5
6							6
7							7
8							8
9							9
10							10
11							11
12							12
13							13
14							14
15							15
16							16
17							17
18							18
19							19
20							20
21							21

EXERCISE 2-5, Concluded

JOURNAL PAGE

	DATE		DESCRIPTION	POST. REF.	DEBIT	CREDIT	
1							1
2							2
3							3
4							4
5							5
6							6
7							7
8							8

EXERCISE 2-6

Unadjusted Trial Balance

EXERCISE 2-7

1. Accounts Payable: ____________________

2. Accounts Receivable: ____________________

3. Cash: ____________________

4. Fees Earned: ____________________

5. Insurance Expense: ____________________

6. Meg Abdel, Drawing: ____________________

7. Supplies Expense: ____________________

EXERCISE 2-8

a. Accounts Payable: ______________________

b. Accounts Receivable: ______________________

d. Billy Eldrod, Capital: ______________________

e. Billy Eldrod, Drawing: ______________________

c. Cash: ______________________

f. Fees Earned: ______________________

g. Office Equipment: ______________________

h. Rent Expense: ______________________

i. Supplies: ______________________

j. Wages Expense: ______________________

EXERCISE 2-9

	Increase	Decrease	Normal Balance
Balance sheet accounts:			
Asset	Debit	**(a)** ________	**(b)** ________
Liability	Credit	**(c)** ________	**(d)** ________
Owner's Equity:			
Capital	**(e)** ________	Debit	**(f)** ________
Drawing	**(g)** ________	**(h)** ________	Debit
Income statement accounts:			
Revenue	**(i)** ________	**(j)** ________	**(k)** ________
Expense	**(l)** ________	Credit	Debit

EXERCISE 2-10

a. ______________________

____

b. ______________________

____

____

EXERCISE 2-11

a. ______________________

____

____

b. ______________________

Name ____________________________________

EXERCISE 2-12

a.

Accounts Payable

b.

Accounts Receivable

c.

Cash

EXERCISE 2-13

JOURNAL

PAGE

DATE		DESCRIPTION	POST. REF.	DEBIT	CREDIT

Name ______________________________

EXERCISE 2-14

a.

JOURNAL PAGE 19

	DATE		DESCRIPTION	POST. REF.	DEBIT	CREDIT	
1							1
2							2
3							3
4							4

b., c., d.

ACCOUNT ACCOUNT NO.

DATE		ITEM	POST. REF.	DEBIT	CREDIT	BALANCE	
						DEBIT	CREDIT

ACCOUNT ACCOUNT NO.

DATE		ITEM	POST. REF.	DEBIT	CREDIT	BALANCE	
						DEBIT	CREDIT

EXERCISE 2-15

a.

JOURNAL PAGE

	DATE		DESCRIPTION	POST. REF.	DEBIT	CREDIT	
1							1
2							2
3							3
4							4
5							5
6							6
7							7
8							8
9							9
10							10
11							11

EXERCISE 2-15, Concluded

b.

Cash

Accounts Payable

Supplies

Fees Earned

Accounts Receivable

EXERCISE 2-16

Unadjusted Trial Balance

EXERCISE 2-17

EXERCISE 2-18

Unadjusted Trial Balance

EXERCISE 2-19

Error	(a) Out of Balance	(b) Difference	(c) Larger Total
1.	yes	$6,150	debit
2.			
3.			
4.			
5.			
6.			
7.			

EXERCISE 2-20

(Optional)

Unadjusted Trial Balance

Name ______________________________

EXERCISE 2-21

JOURNAL PAGE

	DATE		DESCRIPTION	POST. REF.	DEBIT	CREDIT	
1							1
2							2
3							3
4							4
5							5

EXERCISE 2-22

JOURNAL PAGE

	DATE		DESCRIPTION	POST. REF.	DEBIT	CREDIT	
1							1
2							2
3							3
4							4
5							5
6							6
7							7
8							8
9							9

EXERCISE 2-23

a. 1. Net sales: ______________________________

____

2. Total operating expenses: ______________________________

____

b. ______________________________

____

____

____

____

EXERCISE 2-24

a.

Income Statement

	2000	1999	Increase (Decrease) Amount	Increase (Decrease) Percent

b.

Name ______________________________

PROBLEM 2-1 ___

1. and 2.

Cash

Accounts Receivable

Supplies

Prepaid Insurance

Automobiles

PROBLEM 2-1 ___, Continued

Equipment

Notes Payable

Accounts Payable

_________________, Capital

Professional Fees

Rent Expense

Salary Expense

PROBLEM 2-1 ___, Continued

Blueprint Expense

Automobile Expense

Miscellaneous Expense

PROBLEM 2-1 ___, Concluded

3.

Unadjusted Trial Balance

PROBLEM 2-2 ___

1.

JOURNAL

PAGE

DATE		DESCRIPTION	POST. REF.	DEBIT	CREDIT

PROBLEM 2-2 ___, Continued

2.

Cash

Supplies

Accounts Payable

______________________, *Capital*

______________________, *Drawing*

Sales Commissions

PROBLEM 2-2 ___, Continued

Rent Expense

Office Salaries Expense

Automobile Expense

Supplies Expense

Miscellaneous Expense

PROBLEM 2-2 ___, Concluded

3.

Unadjusted Trial Balance

4. a. ______________________

   b. ______________________

   c. ______________________

PROBLEM 2-3 ___

1.

JOURNAL

PAGE *1*

	DATE		DESCRIPTION	POST. REF.	DEBIT	CREDIT	
1							1
2							2
3							3
4							4
5							5
6							6
7							7
8							8
9							9
10							10
11							11
12							12
13							13
14							14
15							15
16							16
17							17
18							18
19							19
20							20
21							21
22							22
23							23
24							24
25							25
26							26
27							27
28							28
29							29
30							30
31							31
32							32
33							33
34							34
35							35
36							36

PROBLEM 2-3 ___, Continued

JOURNAL

PAGE 2

DATE		DESCRIPTION	POST. REF.	DEBIT	CREDIT

Name ______________________________

PROBLEM 2-3 ___, Continued

2.

GENERAL LEDGER

ACCOUNT *Cash* ACCOUNT NO. *11*

DATE		ITEM	POST. REF.	DEBIT	CREDIT	BALANCE DEBIT	BALANCE CREDIT

ACCOUNT *Accounts Receivable* ACCOUNT NO. *12*

DATE		ITEM	POST. REF.	DEBIT	CREDIT	BALANCE DEBIT	BALANCE CREDIT

ACCOUNT *Supplies* ACCOUNT NO. *13*

DATE		ITEM	POST. REF.	DEBIT	CREDIT	BALANCE DEBIT	BALANCE CREDIT

PROBLEM 2-3 ___, Continued

ACCOUNT *Prepaid Insurance* ACCOUNT NO. *14*

DATE		ITEM	POST. REF.	DEBIT	CREDIT	BALANCE	
						DEBIT	CREDIT

ACCOUNT *Equipment* ACCOUNT NO. *16*

DATE		ITEM	POST. REF.	DEBIT	CREDIT	BALANCE	
						DEBIT	CREDIT

ACCOUNT *Truck* ACCOUNT NO. *18*

DATE		ITEM	POST. REF.	DEBIT	CREDIT	BALANCE	
						DEBIT	CREDIT

ACCOUNT *Notes Payable* ACCOUNT NO. *21*

DATE		ITEM	POST. REF.	DEBIT	CREDIT	BALANCE	
						DEBIT	CREDIT

ACCOUNT *Accounts Payable* ACCOUNT NO. *22*

DATE		ITEM	POST. REF.	DEBIT	CREDIT	BALANCE	
						DEBIT	CREDIT

PROBLEM 2-3 ___, Continued

ACCOUNT ______________________, *Capital* ACCOUNT NO. *31*

DATE		ITEM	POST. REF.	DEBIT	CREDIT	BALANCE	
						DEBIT	CREDIT

ACCOUNT ______________________, *Drawing* ACCOUNT NO. *32*

DATE		ITEM	POST. REF.	DEBIT	CREDIT	BALANCE	
						DEBIT	CREDIT

ACCOUNT *Fees Earned* ACCOUNT NO. *41*

DATE		ITEM	POST. REF.	DEBIT	CREDIT	BALANCE	
						DEBIT	CREDIT

PROBLEM 2-3 ___, Continued

ACCOUNT *Wages Expense* ACCOUNT NO. *51*

DATE		ITEM	POST. REF.	DEBIT	CREDIT	BALANCE DEBIT	BALANCE CREDIT

ACCOUNT *Rent Expense* ACCOUNT NO. *53*

DATE		ITEM	POST. REF.	DEBIT	CREDIT	BALANCE DEBIT	BALANCE CREDIT

ACCOUNT *Utilities Expense* ACCOUNT NO. *54*

DATE		ITEM	POST. REF.	DEBIT	CREDIT	BALANCE DEBIT	BALANCE CREDIT

ACCOUNT *Truck Expense* ACCOUNT NO. *55*

DATE		ITEM	POST. REF.	DEBIT	CREDIT	BALANCE DEBIT	BALANCE CREDIT

ACCOUNT *Miscellaneous Expense* ACCOUNT NO. *59*

DATE		ITEM	POST. REF.	DEBIT	CREDIT	BALANCE DEBIT	BALANCE CREDIT

Name ______________________________

PROBLEM 2-3 ___, Concluded

3.

Unadjusted Trial Balance

Name ____________________________________

PROBLEM 2-4 ___

2. and 3.

JOURNAL

PAGE 18

	DATE		DESCRIPTION	POST. REF.	DEBIT	CREDIT	
1							1
2							2
3							3
4							4
5							5
6							6
7							7
8							8
9							9
10							10
11							11
12							12
13							13
14							14
15							15
16							16
17							17
18							18
19							19
20							20
21							21
22							22
23							23
24							24
25							25
26							26
27							27
28							28
29							29
30							30
31							31
32							32
33							33
34							34
35							35
36							36

PROBLEM 2-4 ___, Continued

JOURNAL

PAGE 19

DATE		DESCRIPTION	POST. REF.	DEBIT	CREDIT

Name ______________________________

PROBLEM 2-4 ___, Continued

1. and 3.

ACCOUNT *Cash* ACCOUNT NO. 11

DATE		ITEM	POST. REF.	DEBIT	CREDIT	BALANCE DEBIT	BALANCE CREDIT

ACCOUNT *Accounts Receivable* ACCOUNT NO. 12

DATE		ITEM	POST. REF.	DEBIT	CREDIT	BALANCE DEBIT	BALANCE CREDIT

ACCOUNT *Prepaid Insurance* ACCOUNT NO. 13

DATE		ITEM	POST. REF.	DEBIT	CREDIT	BALANCE DEBIT	BALANCE CREDIT

PROBLEM 2-4 ___, Continued

ACCOUNT *Office Supplies* ACCOUNT NO. *14*

DATE		ITEM	POST. REF.	DEBIT	CREDIT	BALANCE DEBIT	BALANCE CREDIT

ACCOUNT *Land* ACCOUNT NO. *16*

DATE		ITEM	POST. REF.	DEBIT	CREDIT	BALANCE DEBIT	BALANCE CREDIT

ACCOUNT *Accounts Payable* ACCOUNT NO. *21*

DATE		ITEM	POST. REF.	DEBIT	CREDIT	BALANCE DEBIT	BALANCE CREDIT

ACCOUNT *Unearned Rent* ACCOUNT NO. *22*

DATE		ITEM	POST. REF.	DEBIT	CREDIT	BALANCE DEBIT	BALANCE CREDIT

ACCOUNT *Notes Payable* ACCOUNT NO. *23*

DATE		ITEM	POST. REF.	DEBIT	CREDIT	BALANCE DEBIT	BALANCE CREDIT

Name ______________________________

PROBLEM 2-4 ___, Continued

ACCOUNT ______________________, *Capital* ACCOUNT NO. *31*

DATE		ITEM	POST. REF.	DEBIT	CREDIT	BALANCE DEBIT	BALANCE CREDIT

ACCOUNT ______________________, *Drawing* ACCOUNT NO. *32*

DATE		ITEM	POST. REF.	DEBIT	CREDIT	BALANCE DEBIT	BALANCE CREDIT

ACCOUNT *Fees Earned* ACCOUNT NO. *41*

DATE		ITEM	POST. REF.	DEBIT	CREDIT	BALANCE DEBIT	BALANCE CREDIT

ACCOUNT *Salary and Commission Expense* ACCOUNT NO. *51*

DATE		ITEM	POST. REF.	DEBIT	CREDIT	BALANCE DEBIT	BALANCE CREDIT

PROBLEM 2-4 ___, Continued

ACCOUNT *Rent Expense* ACCOUNT NO. 52

DATE		ITEM	POST. REF.	DEBIT	CREDIT	BALANCE DEBIT	BALANCE CREDIT

ACCOUNT *Advertising Expense* ACCOUNT NO. 53

DATE		ITEM	POST. REF.	DEBIT	CREDIT	BALANCE DEBIT	BALANCE CREDIT

ACCOUNT *Automobile Expense* ACCOUNT NO. 54

DATE		ITEM	POST. REF.	DEBIT	CREDIT	BALANCE DEBIT	BALANCE CREDIT

ACCOUNT *Miscellaneous Expense* ACCOUNT NO. 59

DATE		ITEM	POST. REF.	DEBIT	CREDIT	BALANCE DEBIT	BALANCE CREDIT

PROBLEM 2-4 ___, Concluded

4.

Unadjusted Trial Balance

Name ______________________________

PROBLEM 2-5 ___

JOURNAL

PAGE *19*

DATE		DESCRIPTION	POST. REF.	DEBIT	CREDIT
20— May	*1*	*Rent Expense*	*52*	*1,540.00*	
		Cash	*11*		*1,540.00*
	4	*Supplies*	*12*	*149.00*	
		Accounts Payable	*22*		*149.00*
	6	*Advertising Expense*	*54*	*275.00*	
		Cash	*11*		*275.00*
	8	*Cash*	*11*	*1,595.30*	
		Service Revenue	*41*		*1,595.30*
	9	*Prepaid Insurance*	*13*	*144.00*	
		Cash	*11*		*144.00*
	10	*Land*	*16*	*12,000.00*	
		Cash	*11*		*5,500.00*
		Notes Payable	*21*		*6,500.00*
	13	*Accounts Payable*	*22*	*847.20*	
		Cash	*11*		*847.20*
	14	*Miscellaneous Expense*	*58*	*162.10*	
		Cash	*11*		*162.10*
	15	*Wages Expense*	*51*	*1,128.60*	
		Cash	*11*		*1,128.60*
	15	*Cash*	*11*	*1,785.50*	
		Service Revenue	*41*		*1,785.50*
	16	*Tina Reid, Drawing*	*32*	*750.00*	
		Cash	*11*		*750.00*
	17	*Supplies*	*12*	*212.60*	
		Accounts Payable	*22*		*212.60*

PROBLEM 2-5 ___, Continued

JOURNAL

PAGE 20

DATE		DESCRIPTION	POST. REF.	DEBIT	CREDIT
20— May	20	Cash	11	1,662.20	
		Service Revenue	41		1,662.20
	22	Accounts Payable	22	74.20	
		Supplies	12		74.20
	25	Miscellaneous Expense	58	121.40	
		Cash	11		121.40
	25	Cash	11	1,681.30	
		Service Revenue	41		1,681.30
	30	Utilities Expense	53	436.60	
		Cash	11		436.60
	31	Wages Expense	51	1,390.00	
		Cash	11		1,390.00
	31	Tina Reid, Drawing	32	600.00	
		Cash	11		600.00
	31	Cash	11	1,276.10	
		Service Revenue	41		1,276.10

Name ________________________________

PROBLEM 2-5 ___, Continued

1. and 3.

ACCOUNT *Cash* ACCOUNT NO. *11*

DATE		ITEM	POST. REF.	DEBIT	CREDIT	BALANCE DEBIT	BALANCE CREDIT
20— May	1	Balance	√			13,810.50	
	1		19		1,540.00		
	6		19		275.00		
	8		19	1,595.30			
	9		19		144.00		
	10		19		5,500.00		
	13		19		847.20		
	14		19		162.10		
	15		19		1,128.60		
	15		19	1,785.50			
	16		19		750.00		
	20		20	1,662.20			
	25		20		121.40		
	25		20	1,681.30			
	30		20		346.60		
	31		20		1,390.00		
	31		20		600.00		
	31		20	1,276.10		9,006.00	

ACCOUNT *Supplies* ACCOUNT NO. *12*

DATE		ITEM	POST. REF.	DEBIT	CREDIT	BALANCE DEBIT	BALANCE CREDIT
20— May	1	Balance	√			710.50	
	4		19	149.00			
	17		19	212.60			
	22		20		74.20	997.90	

ACCOUNT *Prepaid Insurance* ACCOUNT NO. *13*

DATE		ITEM	POST. REF.	DEBIT	CREDIT	BALANCE DEBIT	BALANCE CREDIT
20— May	1	Balance	√			251.50	
	9		19	14.40		265.90	

PROBLEM 2-5 ___, Continued

ACCOUNT *Land* ACCOUNT NO. *16*

DATE		ITEM	POST. REF.	DEBIT	CREDIT	BALANCE DEBIT	BALANCE CREDIT
20— May	1	Balance	√	14,625.00		14,625.00	
	10		19	1,200.00		15,825.00	

ACCOUNT *Notes Payable* ACCOUNT NO. *21*

DATE		ITEM	POST. REF.	DEBIT	CREDIT	BALANCE DEBIT	BALANCE CREDIT
20— May	10		19		6,500.00		6,500.00

ACCOUNT *Accounts Payable* ACCOUNT NO. *22*

DATE		ITEM	POST. REF.	DEBIT	CREDIT	BALANCE DEBIT	BALANCE CREDIT
20— May	1	Balance	√				1,637.30
	4		19		149.00		
	13		19	847.20			
	17		19		212.60		
	22		20	74.20			1,151.70

ACCOUNT *Tina Reid, Capital* ACCOUNT NO. *31*

DATE		ITEM	POST. REF.	DEBIT	CREDIT	BALANCE DEBIT	BALANCE CREDIT
20— May	1	Balance	√				27,760.20

Name ______________________________

PROBLEM 2-5 ___, Continued

ACCOUNT *Tina Reid, Drawing* ACCOUNT NO. 32

DATE		ITEM	POST. REF.	DEBIT	CREDIT	BALANCE DEBIT	BALANCE CREDIT
20— May	16		19	750.00			
	31		20	600.00		1,350.00	

ACCOUNT *Service Revenue* ACCOUNT NO. 41

DATE		ITEM	POST. REF.	DEBIT	CREDIT	BALANCE DEBIT	BALANCE CREDIT
20— May	8		19		1,595.30		
	15		19		1,785.50		
	20		20		1,662.20		
	25		20		1,681.30		
	31		20		1,276.10		8,000.40

ACCOUNT *Wages Expense* ACCOUNT NO. 51

DATE		ITEM	POST. REF.	DEBIT	CREDIT	BALANCE DEBIT	BALANCE CREDIT
20— May	15		19	1,128.60			
	31		20	1,930.00		3,058.60	

PROBLEM 2-5 ___, Continued

ACCOUNT *Rent Expense* ACCOUNT NO. 52

DATE		ITEM	POST. REF.	DEBIT	CREDIT	BALANCE	
						DEBIT	CREDIT
20— May	1		19	1,540.00		1,540.00	

ACCOUNT *Utilities Expense* ACCOUNT NO. 53

DATE		ITEM	POST. REF.	DEBIT	CREDIT	BALANCE	
						DEBIT	CREDIT
20— May	30		20	436.60		436.60	

ACCOUNT *Advertising Expense* ACCOUNT NO. 54

DATE		ITEM	POST. REF.	DEBIT	CREDIT	BALANCE	
						DEBIT	CREDIT
20— May	6		19	275.00		275.00	

ACCOUNT *Miscellaneous Expense* ACCOUNT NO. 58

DATE		ITEM	POST. REF.	DEBIT	CREDIT	BALANCE	
						DEBIT	CREDIT
20— May	14		19	162.10		162.10	
	25		20	121.40		283.50	

PROBLEM 2-5 ___, Continued

HALLMARK ELECTRONIC REPAIR

Unadjusted Trial Balance

May 31, 20—

Cash	9,006.00	
Supplies	99.79	
Prepaid Insurance	265.90	
Land	15,825.00	
Notes Payable		5,600.00
Accounts Payable		1,151.70
Tina Reid, Capital		27,760.20
Tina Reid, Drawing		1,350.00
Service Revenue		8,000.40
Wages Expense	3,058.60	
Rent Expense	1,540.00	
Utilities Expense	436.60	
Miscellaneous Expense	283.50	
	30,515.39	43,862.30

Name ____________________________________

PROBLEM 2-5 ___, Continued

Verification Schedule

1. Totals of preliminary trial balance: Debit $ ____________
Credit $ ____________

2. Difference between preliminary trial balance totals: $ ____________

3. Errors in trial balance:

____
____
____
____
____
____

4. Errors in account balances:

____
____

5. Errors in posting:

____
____
____
____
____
____
____
____

6. Journal entry:

JOURNAL PAGE *19*

	DATE		DESCRIPTION	POST. REF.	DEBIT	CREDIT	
1							1
2							2
3							3
4							4

PROBLEM 2-5 ___, Concluded

7.

HALLMARK ELECTRONIC REPAIR

Unadjusted Trial Balance

May 31, 20—

PROBLEM 2-6 ___

1.

Corrected Unadjusted Trial Balance

	Debit Balances	Credit Balances
Cash		
Accounts Receivable		
Supplies		
Prepaid Insurance		
Equipment		
Notes Payable		
Accounts Payable		
______________________, *Capital*		
______________________, *Drawing*		
Fees Earned		
Wages Expense		
Rent Expense		
Advertising Expense		
Gas, Electricity, and Water Expense		
Miscellaneous Expense		

2.

Name ______________________________

CONTINUING PROBLEM

2. and 3.

JOURNAL

PAGE *1*

	DATE		DESCRIPTION	POST. REF.	DEBIT	CREDIT	
1							1
2							2
3							3
4							4
5							5
6							6
7							7
8							8
9							9
10							10
11							11
12							12
13							13
14							14
15							15
16							16
17							17
18							18
19							19
20							20
21							21
22							22
23							23
24							24
25							25
26							26
27							27
28							28
29							29
30							30
31							31
32							32
33							33
34							34
35							35
36							36

CONTINUING PROBLEM, Continued

JOURNAL

PAGE 2

	DATE		DESCRIPTION	POST. REF.	DEBIT	CREDIT	
1							1
2							2
3							3
4							4
5							5
6							6
7							7
8							8
9							9
10							10
11							11
12							12
13							13
14							14
15							15
16							16
17							17
18							18
19							19
20							20
21							21
22							22
23							23
24							24
25							25
26							26
27							27
28							28
29							29
30							30
31							31
32							32
33							33
34							34
35							35
36							36

Name ____________________

CONTINUING PROBLEM, Continued

1. and 3.

ACCOUNT *Cash* ACCOUNT NO. *11*

DATE		ITEM	POST. REF.	DEBIT	CREDIT	BALANCE	
						DEBIT	CREDIT

ACCOUNT *Accounts Receivable* ACCOUNT NO. *12*

DATE		ITEM	POST. REF.	DEBIT	CREDIT	BALANCE	
						DEBIT	CREDIT

CONTINUING PROBLEM, Continued

ACCOUNT *Supplies* ACCOUNT NO. *14*

DATE		ITEM	POST. REF.	DEBIT	CREDIT	BALANCE	
						DEBIT	CREDIT

ACCOUNT *Prepaid Insurance* ACCOUNT NO. *15*

DATE		ITEM	POST. REF.	DEBIT	CREDIT	BALANCE	
						DEBIT	CREDIT

ACCOUNT *Office Equipment* ACCOUNT NO. *17*

DATE		ITEM	POST. REF.	DEBIT	CREDIT	BALANCE	
						DEBIT	CREDIT

ACCOUNT *Accumulated Depreciation—Office Equipment* ACCOUNT NO. *18*

DATE		ITEM	POST. REF.	DEBIT	CREDIT	BALANCE	
						DEBIT	CREDIT

(This account is not used in Chapter 2.)

ACCOUNT *Accounts Payable* ACCOUNT NO. *21*

DATE		ITEM	POST. REF.	DEBIT	CREDIT	BALANCE	
						DEBIT	CREDIT

CONTINUING PROBLEM, Continued

ACCOUNT *Wages Payable* ACCOUNT NO. *22*

DATE		ITEM	POST. REF.	DEBIT	CREDIT	BALANCE DEBIT	BALANCE CREDIT

(This account is not used in Chapter 2.)

ACCOUNT *Unearned Revenue* ACCOUNT NO. *23*

DATE		ITEM	POST. REF.	DEBIT	CREDIT	BALANCE DEBIT	BALANCE CREDIT

ACCOUNT *Lee Chang, Capital* ACCOUNT NO. *31*

DATE		ITEM	POST. REF.	DEBIT	CREDIT	BALANCE DEBIT	BALANCE CREDIT

ACCOUNT *Lee Chang, Drawing* ACCOUNT NO. *32*

DATE		ITEM	POST. REF.	DEBIT	CREDIT	BALANCE DEBIT	BALANCE CREDIT

ACCOUNT *Income Summary* ACCOUNT NO. *33*

DATE		ITEM	POST. REF.	DEBIT	CREDIT	BALANCE DEBIT	BALANCE CREDIT

(This account is not used in Chapter 2.)

CONTINUING PROBLEM, Continued

ACCOUNT *Fees Earned* ACCOUNT NO. *41*

DATE		ITEM	POST. REF.	DEBIT	CREDIT	BALANCE	
						DEBIT	CREDIT

ACCOUNT *Wages Expense* ACCOUNT NO. *50*

DATE		ITEM	POST. REF.	DEBIT	CREDIT	BALANCE	
						DEBIT	CREDIT

ACCOUNT *Office Rent Expense* ACCOUNT NO. *51*

DATE		ITEM	POST. REF.	DEBIT	CREDIT	BALANCE	
						DEBIT	CREDIT

ACCOUNT *Equipment Rent Expense* ACCOUNT NO. *52*

DATE		ITEM	POST. REF.	DEBIT	CREDIT	BALANCE	
						DEBIT	CREDIT

CONTINUING PROBLEM, Continued

ACCOUNT *Utilities Expense* ACCOUNT NO. *53*

DATE		ITEM	POST. REF.	DEBIT	CREDIT	BALANCE DEBIT	BALANCE CREDIT

ACCOUNT *Music Expense* ACCOUNT NO. *54*

DATE		ITEM	POST. REF.	DEBIT	CREDIT	BALANCE DEBIT	BALANCE CREDIT

ACCOUNT *Advertising Expense* ACCOUNT NO. *55*

DATE		ITEM	POST. REF.	DEBIT	CREDIT	BALANCE DEBIT	BALANCE CREDIT

ACCOUNT *Supplies Expense* ACCOUNT NO. *56*

DATE		ITEM	POST. REF.	DEBIT	CREDIT	BALANCE DEBIT	BALANCE CREDIT

ACCOUNT *Insurance Expense* ACCOUNT NO. *57*

DATE		ITEM	POST. REF.	DEBIT	CREDIT	BALANCE DEBIT	BALANCE CREDIT

(This account is not used in Chapter 2.)

CONTINUING PROBLEM, Concluded

ACCOUNT *Depreciation Expense* ACCOUNT NO. *58*

DATE		ITEM	POST. REF.	DEBIT	CREDIT	BALANCE	
						DEBIT	CREDIT

(This account is not used in Chapter 2.)

ACCOUNT *Miscellaneous Expense* ACCOUNT NO. *59*

DATE		ITEM	POST. REF.	DEBIT	CREDIT	BALANCE	
						DEBIT	CREDIT

4.

Unadjusted Trial Balance

EXERCISE 3-1

1. A two-year premium paid on a fire insurance policy: ____________________
2. Fees earned but not yet received: ____________________
3. Fees received but not yet earned: ____________________
4. Salary owed but not yet paid: ____________________
5. Subscriptions received in advance by a magazine publisher: ____________________
6. Supplies on hand: ____________________
7. Taxes owed but payable in the following period: ____________________
8. Utilities owed but not yet paid: ____________________

EXERCISE 3-2

Account	Answer
Accounts Receivable	Normally requires adjustment (AR).
Cash...	
Interest Payable	
Interest Receivable	
Joyce Carns, Capital.................	
Land	
Office Equipment	
Prepaid Rent.............................	
Supplies	
Unearned Fees	
Wages Expense.........................	

EXERCISE 3-3

JOURNAL PAGE

	DATE		DESCRIPTION	POST. REF.	DEBIT	CREDIT	
1							1
2							2
3							3

EXERCISE 3-4

____

____

EXERCISE 3-5

a. ______________________________

____

____

b. ______________________________

____

____

EXERCISE 3-6

2. and b.

JOURNAL PAGE

	DATE		DESCRIPTION	POST. REF.	DEBIT	CREDIT	
1							1
2							2
3							3
4							4
5							5
6							6

EXERCISE 3-7

2. and b.

JOURNAL PAGE

	DATE		DESCRIPTION	POST. REF.	DEBIT	CREDIT	
1							1
2							2
3							3
4							4
5							5
6							6

EXERCISE 3-8

JOURNAL PAGE

	DATE		DESCRIPTION	POST. REF.	DEBIT	CREDIT	
1							1
2							2
3							3

EXERCISE 3-9

a. ______________________________

____

____

b. ______________________________

____

____

EXERCISE 3-10

a.

JOURNAL PAGE

	DATE		DESCRIPTION	POST. REF.	DEBIT	CREDIT	
1							1
2							2
3							3

b.

____

____

____

____

EXERCISE 3-11

2. and b.

JOURNAL PAGE

	DATE		DESCRIPTION	POST. REF.	DEBIT	CREDIT	
1							1
2							2
3							3
4							4
5							5
6							6
7							7

EXERCISE 3-12

a. ______________________________

____

b. ______________________________

____

EXERCISE 3-13

2. and b.

JOURNAL PAGE

	DATE		DESCRIPTION	POST. REF.	DEBIT	CREDIT	
1							1
2							2
3							3
4							4
5							5
6							6
7							7

EXERCISE 3-14

____

____

____

EXERCISE 3-15

a. ______________________________

____

____

____

b. ______________________________

____

____

____

Name ______________________________

EXERCISE 3-16

a. ______________________________

____

b. ______________________________

____

____

EXERCISE 3-17

a.

JOURNAL PAGE

	DATE		DESCRIPTION	POST. REF.	DEBIT	CREDIT	
1							1
2							2
3							3
4							4
5							5
6							6
7							7

b. ______________________________

EXERCISE 3-18

JOURNAL PAGE

	DATE		DESCRIPTION	POST. REF.	DEBIT	CREDIT	
1							1
2							2
3							3
4							4
5							5

EXERCISE 3-19

a. ______________________________

b. ______________________________

____

____

EXERCISE 3-20

a. ______________________

b. ______________________

EXERCISE 3-21

____

EXERCISE 3-22

a. ______________________

b. ______________________

EXERCISE 3-23

	Error (a)		Error (b)	
	Overstated	**Understated**	**Overstated**	**Understated**
1. Revenue for the year would be........................	$	$	$	$
2. Expenses for the year would be	$	$	$	$
3. Net income for the year would be....................	$	$	$	$
4. Assets at July 31 would be	$	$	$	$
5. Liabilities at July 31 would be	$	$	$	$
6. Owner's equity at July 31 would be	$	$	$	$

EXERCISE 3-24

____

EXERCISE 3-25

a.

JOURNAL PAGE

	DATE		DESCRIPTION	POST. REF.	DEBIT	CREDIT	
1							1
2							2
3							3

Name ____________________

EXERCISE 3-25, Concluded

2. (1) ____________________

(2) ____________________

EXERCISE 3-26

JOURNAL PAGE

	DATE		DESCRIPTION	POST. REF.	DEBIT	CREDIT	
1							1
2							2
3							3
4							4
5							5
6							6
7							7
8							8
9							9
10							10
11							11
12							12
13							13
14							14

EXERCISE 3-27

EXERCISE 3-27, Concluded
(Optional)

Adjusted Trial Balance

EXERCISE 3-28

a.

b.

c.

EXERCISE 3-29

a. Dell Inc.

	Amount	Percent

b. Gateway, Inc.

	Amount	Percent

c.

Name ______________________________

PROBLEM 3-1 ___

1.

JOURNAL

PAGE

	DATE		DESCRIPTION	POST. REF.	DEBIT	CREDIT	
1							1
2							2
3							3
4							4
5							5
6							6
7							7
8							8
9							9
10							10
11							11
12							12
13							13
14							14
15							15
16							16
17							17
18							18
19							19
20							20

2.

____

____

____

Name ____________________________

PROBLEM 3-2 ___

JOURNAL

PAGE

DATE		DESCRIPTION	POST. REF.	DEBIT	CREDIT

PROBLEM 3-3 ___

JOURNAL

PAGE

	DATE		DESCRIPTION	POST. REF.	DEBIT	CREDIT	
1							1
2							2
3							3
4							4
5							5
6							6
7							7
8							8
9							9
10							10
11							11
12							12
13							13
14							14
15							15
16							16
17							17
18							18
19							19
20							20
21							21
22							22
23							23
24							24
25							25
26							26
27							27
28							28
29							29
30							30
31							31
32							32
33							33
34							34
35							35
36							36

Name ______________________________

PROBLEM 3-4 ___

JOURNAL

PAGE

DATE		DESCRIPTION	POST. REF.	DEBIT	CREDIT

Name ______________________________

PROBLEM 3-5 ___

1.

JOURNAL

PAGE

	DATE		DESCRIPTION	POST. REF.	DEBIT	CREDIT	
1							1
2							2
3							3
4							4
5							5
6							6
7							7
8							8
9							9
10							10
11							11
12							12
13							13
14							14
15							15
16							16
17							17
18							18
19							19
20							20
21							21
22							22
23							23
24							24
25							25
26							26
27							27
28							28
29							29
30							30
31							31
32							32
33							33
34							34
35							35
36							36

PROBLEM 3-5 ___, Concluded

2.

Adjusted Trial Balance

PROBLEM 3-6 ___

1.

JOURNAL

PAGE

	DATE		DESCRIPTION	POST. REF.	DEBIT	CREDIT	
1							1
2							2
3							3
4							4
5							5
6							6
7							7
8							8
9							9
10							10
11							11
12							12
13							13
14							14
15							15
16							16
17							17
18							18
19							19
20							20
21							21
22							22
23							23
24							24
25							25
26							26
27							27
28							28
29							29
30							30
31							31
32							32
33							33
34							34
35							35
36							36

PROBLEM 3-6 ___, Concluded

2.

	Net Income	Total Assets	Total Liabilities	Total Owner's Equity
Reported amounts	$	$	$	$
Corrections:				
Adjustment (a)				
Adjustment (b)				
Adjustment (c)				
Adjustment (d)				
Corrected amounts	$	$	$	$

Name ______________________________

CONTINUING PROBLEM

1.

JOURNAL

PAGE 3

	DATE		DESCRIPTION	POST. REF.	DEBIT	CREDIT	
1							1
2							2
3							3
4							4
5							5
6							6
7							7
8							8
9							9
10							10
11							11
12							12
13							13
14							14
15							15
16							16
17							17
18							18
19							19
20							20
21							21
22							22
23							23
24							24
25							25
26							26
27							27
28							28
29							29
30							30
31							31
32							32
33							33
34							34
35							35
36							36

CONTINUING PROBLEM, Continued

2.

ACCOUNT *Cash* ACCOUNT NO. *11*

DATE		ITEM	POST. REF.	DEBIT	CREDIT	BALANCE	
						DEBIT	CREDIT

ACCOUNT *Accounts Receivable* ACCOUNT NO. *12*

DATE		ITEM	POST. REF.	DEBIT	CREDIT	BALANCE	
						DEBIT	CREDIT

Name ______________________________

CONTINUING PROBLEM, Continued

ACCOUNT *Supplies* ACCOUNT NO. *14*

DATE		ITEM	POST. REF.	DEBIT	CREDIT	BALANCE DEBIT	BALANCE CREDIT

ACCOUNT *Prepaid Insurance* ACCOUNT NO. *15*

DATE		ITEM	POST. REF.	DEBIT	CREDIT	BALANCE DEBIT	BALANCE CREDIT

ACCOUNT *Office Equipment* ACCOUNT NO. *17*

DATE		ITEM	POST. REF.	DEBIT	CREDIT	BALANCE DEBIT	BALANCE CREDIT

ACCOUNT *Accumulated Depreciation—Office Equipment* ACCOUNT NO. *18*

DATE		ITEM	POST. REF.	DEBIT	CREDIT	BALANCE DEBIT	BALANCE CREDIT

ACCOUNT *Accounts Payable* ACCOUNT NO. *21*

DATE		ITEM	POST. REF.	DEBIT	CREDIT	BALANCE DEBIT	BALANCE CREDIT

CONTINUING PROBLEM, Continued

ACCOUNT *Wages Payable* ACCOUNT NO. *22*

DATE		ITEM	POST. REF.	DEBIT	CREDIT	BALANCE DEBIT	BALANCE CREDIT

ACCOUNT *Unearned Revenue* ACCOUNT NO. *23*

DATE		ITEM	POST. REF.	DEBIT	CREDIT	BALANCE DEBIT	BALANCE CREDIT

ACCOUNT *Lee Chang, Capital* ACCOUNT NO. *31*

DATE		ITEM	POST. REF.	DEBIT	CREDIT	BALANCE DEBIT	BALANCE CREDIT

ACCOUNT *Lee Chang, Drawing* ACCOUNT NO. *32*

DATE		ITEM	POST. REF.	DEBIT	CREDIT	BALANCE DEBIT	BALANCE CREDIT

ACCOUNT *Income Summary* ACCOUNT NO. *33*

DATE		ITEM	POST. REF.	DEBIT	CREDIT	BALANCE DEBIT	BALANCE CREDIT

CONTINUING PROBLEM, Continued

ACCOUNT *Fees Earned* ACCOUNT NO. *41*

DATE		ITEM	POST. REF.	DEBIT	CREDIT	BALANCE	
						DEBIT	CREDIT

ACCOUNT *Wages Expense* ACCOUNT NO. *50*

DATE		ITEM	POST. REF.	DEBIT	CREDIT	BALANCE	
						DEBIT	CREDIT

ACCOUNT *Office Rent Expense* ACCOUNT NO. *51*

DATE		ITEM	POST. REF.	DEBIT	CREDIT	BALANCE	
						DEBIT	CREDIT

ACCOUNT *Equipment Rent Expense* ACCOUNT NO. *52*

DATE		ITEM	POST. REF.	DEBIT	CREDIT	BALANCE	
						DEBIT	CREDIT

CONTINUING PROBLEM, Continued

ACCOUNT *Utilities Expense* ACCOUNT NO. *53*

DATE		ITEM	POST. REF.	DEBIT	CREDIT	BALANCE DEBIT	BALANCE CREDIT

ACCOUNT *Music Expense* ACCOUNT NO. *54*

DATE		ITEM	POST. REF.	DEBIT	CREDIT	BALANCE DEBIT	BALANCE CREDIT

ACCOUNT *Advertising Expense* ACCOUNT NO. *55*

DATE		ITEM	POST. REF.	DEBIT	CREDIT	BALANCE DEBIT	BALANCE CREDIT

ACCOUNT *Supplies Expense* ACCOUNT NO. *56*

DATE		ITEM	POST. REF.	DEBIT	CREDIT	BALANCE DEBIT	BALANCE CREDIT

ACCOUNT *Insurance Expense* ACCOUNT NO. *57*

DATE		ITEM	POST. REF.	DEBIT	CREDIT	BALANCE DEBIT	BALANCE CREDIT

CONTINUING PROBLEM, Continued

ACCOUNT *Depreciation Expense* ACCOUNT NO. *58*

DATE		ITEM	POST. REF.	DEBIT	CREDIT	BALANCE	
						DEBIT	CREDIT

ACCOUNT *Miscellaneous Expense* ACCOUNT NO. *59*

DATE		ITEM	POST. REF.	DEBIT	CREDIT	BALANCE	
						DEBIT	CREDIT

CONTINUING PROBLEM, Concluded

3.

Adjusted Trial Balance

EXERCISE 4-1

1. Accounts Payable: ______________________
2. Accounts Receivable: ______________________
3. Cash: ______________________
4. Dean Pinkerton, Drawing: ______________________
5. Fees Earned: ______________________
6. Supplies: ______________________
7. Unearned Rent: ______________________
8. Utilities Expense: ______________________
9. Wages Expense: ______________________
10. Wages Payable: ______________________

EXERCISE 4-2

1. Accounts Payable: ______________________
2. Equipment: ______________________
3. Fees Earned: ______________________
4. Insurance Expense: ______________________
5. Prepaid Advertising: ______________________
6. Prepaid Insurance: ______________________
7. Rent Revenue: ______________________
8. Salary Expense: ______________________
9. Salary Payable: ______________________
10. Supplies: ______________________
11. Supplies Expense: ______________________
12. Unearned Rent: ______________________

EXERCISE 4-3

Income Statement

Statement of Owner's Equity

Name ______________________

EXERCISE 4-3, Concluded

Balance Sheet

EXERCISE 4-4

Income Statement

Statement of Owner's Equity

Name ____________________

EXERCISE 4-4, Concluded

Balance Sheet

EXERCISE 4-5

Income Statement

EXERCISE 4-6

Income Statement

EXERCISE 4-7

a.

Income Statement

b.

EXERCISE 4-8

Statement of Owner's Equity

EXERCISE 4-9

Statement of Owner's Equity

EXERCISE 4-10

1. Accounts receivable: ______________________
2. Building: ______________________
3. Cash: ______________________
4. Equipment: ______________________
5. Prepaid rent: ______________________
6. Supplies: ______________________

EXERCISE 4-11

Name ______________________

EXERCISE 4-12

Balance Sheet

EXERCISE 4-13

Name ______________________

EXERCISE 4-13, Concluded

Balance Sheet

EXERCISE 4-14

a. Accounts Receivable: ______________________

b. Accumulated Depreciation—Equipment: ______________________

c. Depreciation Expense—Equipment: ______________________

d. Equipment: ______________________

e. Erin Dowley, Capital: ______________________

f. Erin Dowley, Drawing: ______________________

g. Fees Earned: ______________________

h. Land: ______________________

i. Supplies: ______________________

j. Supplies Expense: ______________________

k. Wages Expense: ______________________

l. Wages Payable: ______________________

EXERCISE 4-15

EXERCISE 4-16

a.

JOURNAL PAGE

	DATE		DESCRIPTION	POST. REF.	DEBIT	CREDIT	
1							1
2							2
3							3
4							4
5							5
6							6

b. ______________________

Name ______________________________

EXERCISE 4-17

JOURNAL

PAGE

	DATE		DESCRIPTION	POST. REF.	DEBIT	CREDIT	
1							1
2							2
3							3
4							4
5							5
6							6
7							7
8							8
9							9
10							10
11							11
12							12
13							13
14							14

EXERCISE 4-18

a. Accounts Payable: ______________________________

b. Accumulated Depreciation: ______________________________

c. Bo Erath, Capital: ______________________________

d. Bo Erath, Drawing: ______________________________

e. Cash: ______________________________

f. Depreciation Expense: ______________________________

g. Fees Earned: ______________________________

h. Office Equipment: ______________________________

i. Salaries Expense: ______________________________

j. Salaries Payable: ______________________________

k. Supplies: ______________________________

EXERCISE 4-19

Post-Closing Trial Balance

Name ______________________________

EXERCISE 4-20

1. ______________________
2. ______________________
3. ______________________
4. ______________________
5. ______________________
6. ______________________
7. ______________________
8. ______________________
9. ______________________
10. ______________________

APPENDIX EXERCISE 4-21

1. ______________________
2. ______________________
3. ______________________
4. ______________________
5. ______________________
6. ______________________
7. ______________________
8. ______________________
9. ______________________
10. ______________________

Name ______________________

APPENDIX EXERCISE 4-22

	A	B	C	D	E	F	G	H	I	J	K
1			Homeland Security Services Co.								
2			End-of-Period Spreadsheet (Work Sheet)								
3			For the Year Ended October 31, 2010								
4		Unadjusted				Adjusted		Income		Balance	
5		Trial Balance		Adjustments		Trial Balance		Statement		Sheet	
6	**Account Title**	Dr.	Cr.	Dr.	Cr.	Dr.	Cr.	Dr.	Cr.	Dr.	Cr.
7	Cash	6									
8	Accounts Receivable	40									
9	Supplies	4									
10	Prepaid Insurance	6									
11	Land	50									
12	Equipment	20									
13	Accumulated Depr. — Equip.		2								
14	Accounts Payable		18								
15	Wages Payable		0								
16	Gloria Millard, Capital		85								
17	Gloria Millard, Drawing	4									
18	Fees Earned		45								
19	Wages Expense	10									
20	Rent Expense	6									
21	Insurance Expense	0									
22	Utilities Expense	3									
23	Depreciation Expense	0									
24	Supplies Expense	0									
25	Miscellaneous Expense	1									
26	Totals	150	150								
27											
28											
29											
30											
31											
32											

Name ______________________

APPENDIX EXERCISE 4-23

	A	B	C	D	E	F	G	H	I	J	K
1			Homeland Security Services Co.								
2			End-of-Period Spreadsheet (Work Sheet)								
3			For the Year Ended October 31, 2010								
4		Unadjusted				Adjusted		Income		Balance	
5		Trial Balance		Adjustments		Trial Balance		Statement		Sheet	
6	**Account Title**	Dr.	Cr.	Dr.	Cr.	Dr.	Cr.	Dr.	Cr.	Dr.	Cr.
7	Cash					6					
8	Accounts Receivable					44					
9	Supplies					1					
10	Prepaid Insurance					1					
11	Land					50					
12	Equipment					20					
13	Accumulated Depr. — Equip.						4				
14	Accounts Payable						18				
15	Wages Payable						2				
16	Gloria Millard, Capital						85				
17	Gloria Millard, Drawing					4					
18	Fees Earned						49				
19	Wages Expense					12					
20	Rent Expense					6					
21	Insurance Expense					5					
22	Utilities Expense					3					
23	Supplies Expense					3					
24	Depreciation Expense					2					
25	Miscellaneous Expense					1					
26	Totals					158	158				
27	Net income (loss)										
28											
29											
30											
31											
32											

APPENDIX EXERCISE 4-24

Income Statement

Statement of Owner's Equity

Name ______________________

APPENDIX EXERCISE 4-24, Concluded

Balance Sheet

APPENDIX EXERCISE 4-25

JOURNAL

PAGE

	DATE		DESCRIPTION	POST. REF.	DEBIT	CREDIT	
1							1
2							2
3							3
4							4
5							5
6							6
7							7
8							8
9							9
10							10
11							11
12							12
13							13
14							14
15							15
16							16
17							17
18							18
19							19
20							20

Name ____________________

APPENDIX EXERCISE 4-26

JOURNAL

PAGE

	DATE		DESCRIPTION	POST. REF.	DEBIT	CREDIT	
1							1
2							2
3							3
4							4
5							5
6							6
7							7
8							8
9							9
10							10
11							11
12							12
13							13
14							14
15							15
16							16
17							17
18							18
19							19
20							20

EXERCISE 4-27

a.

	December 31,	
	2007	**2006**
____________	______	______
____________	______	______
Working capital	______	______
Current ratio	______	______

b.

EXERCISE 4-28

a.

	December 31,	
	2007	**2006**
____________	______	______
____________	______	______
Working capital	______	______
Current ratio	______	______

b.

Name ______________________________

PROBLEM 4-1 ___

1.

Income Statement

2.

Statement of Owner's Equity

Name ______________________________

PROBLEM 4-1 ___, Continued

3.

Balance Sheet

Name ______________________________

PROBLEM 4-1 ___, Continued

4.

JOURNAL

PAGE

	DATE		DESCRIPTION	POST. REF.	DEBIT	CREDIT	
1							1
2							2
3							3
4							4
5							5
6							6
7							7
8							8
9							9
10							10
11							11
12							12
13							13
14							14
15							15
16							16
17							17
18							18
19							19
20							20
21							21
22							22
23							23
24							24
25							25
26							26
27							27
28							28
29							29
30							30
31							31
32							32
33							33
34							34
35							35
36							36

PROBLEM 4-1 ___, Concluded

5.

Post-Closing Trial Balance

Name ____________________

PROBLEM 4-2 ___

1.

Income Statement

Statement of Owner's Equity

Name ______________________

PROBLEM 4-2 ___, Continued

Balance Sheet

PROBLEM 4-2 ___, Concluded

2.

JOURNAL

PAGE

	DATE		DESCRIPTION	POST. REF.	DEBIT	CREDIT	
1							1
2							2
3							3
4							4
5							5
6							6
7							7
8							8
9							9
10							10
11							11
12							12
13							13
14							14
15							15
16							16
17							17
18							18
19							19
20							20
21							21

3.

PROBLEM 4-3 ___

1.

Cash

Laundry Supplies

Prepaid Insurance

Laundry Equipment

Accumulated Depreciation

Accounts Payable

Wages Payable

______________________, Capital

PROBLEM 4-3 ___, Continued

________________________, Drawing

Income Summary

Laundry Revenue

Wages Expense

Rent Expense

Utilities Expense

Depreciation Expense

Laundry Supplies Expense

Insurance Expense

Miscellaneous Expense

Name ______________________

PROBLEM 4-3 ___, Continued

2. Optional (Appendix)

	A	B	C	D	E	F	G	H	I	J	K
1											
2			End-of-Period Spreadsheet (Work Sheet)								
3											
4		Unadjusted				Adjusted		Income		Balance	
5		Trial Balance		Adjustments		Trial Balance		Statement		Sheet	
6	Account Title	Dr.	Cr.	Dr.	Cr.	Dr.	Cr.	Dr.	Cr.	Dr.	Cr.
7											
8											
9											
10											
11											
12											
13											
14											
15											
16											
17											
18											
19											
20											
21											
22											
23											
24											
25											
26											
27											
28											
29											
30											

PROBLEM 4-3 ___, Continued

3.

JOURNAL

PAGE

DATE		DESCRIPTION	POST. REF.	DEBIT	CREDIT
		Adjusting Entries			

PROBLEM 4-3 ___, Continued

4.

Adjusted Trial Balance

PROBLEM 4-3 ___, Continued

5.

Income Statement

Statement of Owner's Equity

Name ______________________

PROBLEM 4-3 ___, Continued

Balance Sheet

PROBLEM 4-3 ___, Concluded

6.

JOURNAL

PAGE

	DATE		DESCRIPTION	POST. REF.	DEBIT	CREDIT	
1			*Closing Entries*				1
2							2
3							3
4							4
5							5
6							6
7							7
8							8
9							9
10							10
11							11
12							12
13							13
14							14
15							15
16							16
17							17
18							18
19							19

7.

Post-Closing Trial Balance

Name ____________________ *Chapter 4*

PROBLEM 4-4 ___

1. Optional (Appendix)

	A	B	C	D	E	F	G	H	I	J	K
1											
2			End-of-Period Spreadsheet (Work Sheet)								
3											
4		Unadjusted				Adjusted		Income		Balance	
5		Trial Balance		Adjustments		Trial Balance		Statement		Sheet	
6	**Account Title**	Dr.	Cr.	Dr.	Cr.	Dr.	Cr.	Dr.	Cr.	Dr.	Cr.
7	Cash	26,870									
8	Accounts Receivable	10,900									
9	Supplies	3,050									
10	Prepaid Insurance	4,800									
11	Land	50,000									
12	Building	57,500									
13	Accum. Depr.—Building		23,400								
14	Equipment	32,000									
15	Accum. Depr.—Equipment		10,200								
16	Accounts Payable		3,350								
17	Wages Payable										
18	Unearned Rent		2,700								
19	Rafael Cagle, Capital		123,000								
20	Rafael Cagle, Drawing	2,000									
21	Service Revenue		35,000								
22	Rent Revenue										
23	Wages Expense	5,000									
24	Supplies Expense										
25	Rent Expense	2,500									
26	Depr. Exp,—Buildings										
27	Utilities Expense	1,650									
28	Depr. Exp.—Equipment										
29	Insurance Expense										
30	Misc. Expense	1,380									
31		197,650	197,650								
32											
33											
34											

PROBLEM 4-4 ___, Continued

2.

JOURNAL PAGE *26*

	DATE		DESCRIPTION	POST. REF.	DEBIT	CREDIT	
1			*Adjusting Entries*				1
2							2
3							3
4							4
5							5
6							6
7							7
8							8
9							9
10							10
11							11
12							12
13							13
14							14
15							15
16							16
17							17
18							18
19							19
20							20
21							21
22							22
23							23
24							24
25							25
26							26
27							27
28							28
29							29
30							30
31							31
32							32
33							33
34							34
35							35
36							36

PROBLEM 4-4 ___, Continued

3.

Adjusted Trial Balance

PROBLEM 4-4 ___, Continued

4.

Income Statement

Statement of Owner's Equity

Name ______________________

PROBLEM 4-4 ___, Continued

Balance Sheet

PROBLEM 4-4 ___, Continued

5.

JOURNAL

PAGE *27*

DATE		DESCRIPTION	POST. REF.	DEBIT	CREDIT
		Closing Entries			

PROBLEM 4-4 ___, Continued

6.

Post-Closing Trial Balance

PROBLEM 4-4 ___, Continued

2. and 5.

ACCOUNT *Cash* ACCOUNT NO. *11*

DATE		ITEM	POST. REF.	DEBIT	CREDIT	BALANCE	
						DEBIT	CREDIT
2010 July	1	Balance	√			6,000.00	
	3		23		2,500.00	3,500.00	
	4		23	5,000.00		8,500.00	
	5		23		400.00	8,100.00	
	7		23	3,200.00		11,300.00	
	8		23	5,900.00		17,200.00	
	8		23		4,500.00	12,700.00	
	8		23	9,400.00		22,100.00	
	10		24		500.00	21,600.00	
	12		24		2,400.00	19,200.00	
	15		24	7,800.00		27,000.00	
	16		24		1,000.00	26,000.00	
	19		24		2,100.00	23,900.00	
	22		24		1,200.00	22,700.00	
	22		24	8,100.00		30,800.00	
	24		25		800.00	30,000.00	
	26		25		2,600.00	27,400.00	
	30		25		350.00	27,050.00	
	30		25		600.00	26,450.00	
	31		25		1,000.00	25,450.00	
	31		25	2,200.00		27,650.00	
	31		25		780.00	26,870.00	

PROBLEM 4-4 ___, Continued

ACCOUNT *Accounts Receivable* ACCOUNT NO. 12

DATE		ITEM	POST. REF.	DEBIT	CREDIT	BALANCE DEBIT	BALANCE CREDIT
2010 July	1	Balance	√			12,500.00	
	7		23		3,200.00	9,300.00	
	8		23		5,900.00	3,400.00	
	22		24	7,500.00		10,900.00	

ACCOUNT *Supplies* ACCOUNT NO. 13

DATE		ITEM	POST. REF.	DEBIT	CREDIT	BALANCE DEBIT	BALANCE CREDIT
2010 July	1	Balance	√			1,750.00	
	10		24	500.00		2,250.00	
	27		25	800.00		3,050.00	

ACCOUNT *Prepaid Insurance* ACCOUNT NO. 14

DATE		ITEM	POST. REF.	DEBIT	CREDIT	BALANCE DEBIT	BALANCE CREDIT
2010 July	1	Balance	√			3,600.00	
	22		24	1,200.00		4,800.00	

ACCOUNT *Land* ACCOUNT NO. 15

DATE		ITEM	POST. REF.	DEBIT	CREDIT	BALANCE DEBIT	BALANCE CREDIT
2010 July	1	Balance	√			50,000.00	

PROBLEM 4-4 ___, Continued

ACCOUNT *Building* ACCOUNT NO. *16*

DATE		ITEM	POST. REF.	DEBIT	CREDIT	BALANCE DEBIT	BALANCE CREDIT
2010 July	1	Balance	√			57,500.00	

ACCOUNT *Accumulated Depreciation—Building* ACCOUNT NO. *17*

DATE		ITEM	POST. REF.	DEBIT	CREDIT	BALANCE DEBIT	BALANCE CREDIT
2010 July	1	Balance	√				23,400.00

ACCOUNT *Equipment* ACCOUNT NO. *18*

DATE		ITEM	POST. REF.	DEBIT	CREDIT	BALANCE DEBIT	BALANCE CREDIT
2010 July	1	Balance	√			29,250.00	
	3		23	2,750.00		32,000.00	

ACCOUNT *Accumulated Depreciation—Equipment* ACCOUNT NO. *19*

DATE		ITEM	POST. REF.	DEBIT	CREDIT	BALANCE DEBIT	BALANCE CREDIT
2010 July	1	Balance	√				10,200.00

PROBLEM 4-4 ___, Continued

ACCOUNT *Accounts Payable* ACCOUNT NO. 21

DATE		ITEM	POST. REF.	DEBIT	CREDIT	BALANCE DEBIT	BALANCE CREDIT
2010 July	1	Balance	√				6,300.00
	3		23		2,750.00		9,050.00
	8		23	4,500.00			4,550.00
	19		24	2,100.00			2,450.00
	31		25		900.00		3,350.00

ACCOUNT *Wages Payable* ACCOUNT NO. 22

DATE		ITEM	POST. REF.	DEBIT	CREDIT	BALANCE DEBIT	BALANCE CREDIT

ACCOUNT *Unearned Rent* ACCOUNT NO. 23

DATE		ITEM	POST. REF.	DEBIT	CREDIT	BALANCE DEBIT	BALANCE CREDIT
2010 July	1	Balance	√				2,700.00

ACCOUNT *Rafael Cagle, Capital* ACCOUNT NO. 31

DATE		ITEM	POST. REF.	DEBIT	CREDIT	BALANCE DEBIT	BALANCE CREDIT
2010 July	1	Balance	√				118,000.00
	4	23	23		5,000.00		123,000.00

PROBLEM 4-4 ___, Continued

ACCOUNT *Rafael Cagle, Drawing* ACCOUNT NO. *32*

DATE		ITEM	POST. REF.	DEBIT	CREDIT	BALANCE DEBIT	BALANCE CREDIT
2010 July	16		24	1,000.00		1,000.00	
	31		25	1,000.00		2,000.00	

ACCOUNT *Income Summary* ACCOUNT NO. *33*

DATE		ITEM	POST. REF.	DEBIT	CREDIT	BALANCE DEBIT	BALANCE CREDIT

ACCOUNT *Service Revenue* ACCOUNT NO. *41*

DATE		ITEM	POST. REF.	DEBIT	CREDIT	BALANCE DEBIT	BALANCE CREDIT
2010 July	8		23		9,400.00		9,400.00
	15		24		7,800.00		17,200.00
	22		24		8,100.00		25,300.00
	22		24		7,500.00		32,800.00
	31		25		2,200.00		35,000.00

PROBLEM 4-4 ___, Concluded

ACCOUNT *Miscellaneous Expense* ACCOUNT NO. 59

DATE		ITEM	POST. REF.	DEBIT	CREDIT	BALANCE	
						DEBIT	CREDIT
2010 July	30		25	600.00		600.00	
	31		25	780.00		1,380.00	

Name ______________________

PROBLEM 4-5 ___

2. Optional (Appendix)

	A	B	C	D	E	F	G	H	I	J	K
1											
2			End-of-Period Spreadsheet (Work Sheet)								
3											
4		Unadjusted				Adjusted		Income		Balance	
5		Trial Balance		Adjustments		Trial Balance		Statement		Sheet	
6	Account Title	Dr.	Cr.	Dr.	Cr.	Dr.	Cr.	Dr.	Cr.	Dr.	Cr.
7											
8											
9											
10											
11											
12											
13											
14											
15											
16											
17											
18											
19											
20											
21											
22											
23											
24											
25											
26											
27											
28											
29											
30											
31											
32											

PROBLEM 4-5 ___, Continued

3.

JOURNAL

PAGE *26*

DATE		DESCRIPTION	POST. REF.	DEBIT	CREDIT
		Adjusting Entries			

PROBLEM 4-5 ___, Continued

4.

Adjusted Trial Balance

PROBLEM 4-5 ___, Continued

5.

Income Statement

Statement of Owner's Equity

Name ______________________________ *Chapter 4*

PROBLEM 4-5 ___, Continued

Balance Sheet

PROBLEM 4-5 ___, Continued

1., 3., and 6.

ACCOUNT *Cash* ACCOUNT NO. *11*

DATE		ITEM	POST. REF.	DEBIT	CREDIT	BALANCE	
						DEBIT	CREDIT

ACCOUNT *Supplies* ACCOUNT NO. *13*

DATE		ITEM	POST. REF.	DEBIT	CREDIT	BALANCE	
						DEBIT	CREDIT

ACCOUNT *Prepaid Insurance* ACCOUNT NO. *14*

DATE		ITEM	POST. REF.	DEBIT	CREDIT	BALANCE	
						DEBIT	CREDIT

ACCOUNT *Equipment* ACCOUNT NO. *16*

DATE		ITEM	POST. REF.	DEBIT	CREDIT	BALANCE	
						DEBIT	CREDIT

ACCOUNT *Accumulated Depreciation—Equipment* ACCOUNT NO. *17*

DATE		ITEM	POST. REF.	DEBIT	CREDIT	BALANCE	
						DEBIT	CREDIT

PROBLEM 4-5 ___, Continued

ACCOUNT *Trucks* ACCOUNT NO. *18*

DATE		ITEM	POST. REF.	DEBIT	CREDIT	BALANCE DEBIT	BALANCE CREDIT

ACCOUNT *Accumulated Depreciation—Trucks* ACCOUNT NO. *19*

DATE		ITEM	POST. REF.	DEBIT	CREDIT	BALANCE DEBIT	BALANCE CREDIT

ACCOUNT *Accounts Payable* ACCOUNT NO. *21*

DATE		ITEM	POST. REF.	DEBIT	CREDIT	BALANCE DEBIT	BALANCE CREDIT

ACCOUNT *Wages Payable* ACCOUNT NO. *22*

DATE		ITEM	POST. REF.	DEBIT	CREDIT	BALANCE DEBIT	BALANCE CREDIT

ACCOUNT ____________________, *Capital* ACCOUNT NO. *31*

DATE		ITEM	POST. REF.	DEBIT	CREDIT	BALANCE DEBIT	BALANCE CREDIT

ACCOUNT ____________________, *Drawing* ACCOUNT NO. *32*

DATE		ITEM	POST. REF.	DEBIT	CREDIT	BALANCE DEBIT	BALANCE CREDIT

PROBLEM 4-5 ___, Continued

ACCOUNT *Income Summary* ACCOUNT NO. *33*

DATE		ITEM	POST. REF.	DEBIT	CREDIT	BALANCE DEBIT	BALANCE CREDIT

ACCOUNT *Service Revenue* ACCOUNT NO. *41*

DATE		ITEM	POST. REF.	DEBIT	CREDIT	BALANCE DEBIT	BALANCE CREDIT

ACCOUNT *Wages Expense* ACCOUNT NO. *51*

DATE		ITEM	POST. REF.	DEBIT	CREDIT	BALANCE DEBIT	BALANCE CREDIT

ACCOUNT *Supplies Expense* ACCOUNT NO. *52*

DATE		ITEM	POST. REF.	DEBIT	CREDIT	BALANCE DEBIT	BALANCE CREDIT

ACCOUNT *Rent Expense* ACCOUNT NO. *53*

DATE		ITEM	POST. REF.	DEBIT	CREDIT	BALANCE DEBIT	BALANCE CREDIT

Name ____________________

PROBLEM 4-5 ___, Continued

ACCOUNT *Depreciation Expense—Equipment* ACCOUNT NO. *54*

DATE		ITEM	POST. REF.	DEBIT	CREDIT	BALANCE	
						DEBIT	CREDIT

ACCOUNT *Truck Expense* ACCOUNT NO. *55*

DATE		ITEM	POST. REF.	DEBIT	CREDIT	BALANCE	
						DEBIT	CREDIT

ACCOUNT *Depreciation Expense—Trucks* ACCOUNT NO. *56*

DATE		ITEM	POST. REF.	DEBIT	CREDIT	BALANCE	
						DEBIT	CREDIT

ACCOUNT *Insurance Expense* ACCOUNT NO. *57*

DATE		ITEM	POST. REF.	DEBIT	CREDIT	BALANCE	
						DEBIT	CREDIT

ACCOUNT *Miscellaneous Expense* ACCOUNT NO. *59*

DATE		ITEM	POST. REF.	DEBIT	CREDIT	BALANCE	
						DEBIT	CREDIT

PROBLEM 4-5 ___, Concluded

6.

JOURNAL PAGE *27*

	DATE		DESCRIPTION	POST. REF.	DEBIT	CREDIT	
1			*Closing Entries*				1
2							2
3							3
4							4
5							5
6							6
7							7
8							8
9							9
10							10
11							11
12							12
13							13
14							14
15							15
16							16
17							17
18							18
19							19
20							20

7.

Post-Closing Trial Balance

Name ______________________________

PROBLEM 4-6 ___

1. and 2.

JOURNAL

PAGE *1*

DATE		DESCRIPTION	POST. REF.	DEBIT	CREDIT

PROBLEM 4-6 ___, Continued

JOURNAL

PAGE 2

	DATE		DESCRIPTION	POST. REF.	DEBIT	CREDIT	
1							1
2							2
3							3
4							4
5							5
6							6
7							7
8							8
9							9
10							10
11							11
12							12
13							13
14							14
15							15
16							16
17							17
18							18
19							19
20							20
21							21
22							22
23							23
24							24
25							25
26							26
27							27
28							28
29							29
30							30
31							31
32							32
33							33
34							34
35							35
36							36

PROBLEM 4-6 ___, Continued

2., 6., and 9.

ACCOUNT *Cash* ACCOUNT NO. *11*

DATE		ITEM	POST. REF.	DEBIT	CREDIT	BALANCE	
						DEBIT	CREDIT

ACCOUNT *Accounts Receivable* ACCOUNT NO. *12*

DATE		ITEM	POST. REF.	DEBIT	CREDIT	BALANCE	
						DEBIT	CREDIT

PROBLEM 4-6 ___, Continued

ACCOUNT *Supplies* ACCOUNT NO. *14*

DATE		ITEM	POST. REF.	DEBIT	CREDIT	BALANCE DEBIT	BALANCE CREDIT

ACCOUNT *Prepaid Rent* ACCOUNT NO. *15*

DATE		ITEM	POST. REF.	DEBIT	CREDIT	BALANCE DEBIT	BALANCE CREDIT

ACCOUNT *Prepaid Insurance* ACCOUNT NO. *16*

DATE		ITEM	POST. REF.	DEBIT	CREDIT	BALANCE DEBIT	BALANCE CREDIT

ACCOUNT *Office Equipment* ACCOUNT NO. *18*

DATE		ITEM	POST. REF.	DEBIT	CREDIT	BALANCE DEBIT	BALANCE CREDIT

ACCOUNT *Accumulated Depreciation* ACCOUNT NO. *19*

DATE		ITEM	POST. REF.	DEBIT	CREDIT	BALANCE DEBIT	BALANCE CREDIT

PROBLEM 4-6 ___, Continued

ACCOUNT *Accounts Payable* ACCOUNT NO. *21*

DATE		ITEM	POST. REF.	DEBIT	CREDIT	BALANCE	
						DEBIT	CREDIT

ACCOUNT *Salaries Payable* ACCOUNT NO. *22*

DATE		ITEM	POST. REF.	DEBIT	CREDIT	BALANCE	
						DEBIT	CREDIT

ACCOUNT *Unearned Fees* ACCOUNT NO. *23*

DATE		ITEM	POST. REF.	DEBIT	CREDIT	BALANCE	
						DEBIT	CREDIT

ACCOUNT ______________________, *Capital* ACCOUNT NO. *31*

DATE		ITEM	POST. REF.	DEBIT	CREDIT	BALANCE	
						DEBIT	CREDIT

ACCOUNT ______________________, *Drawing* ACCOUNT NO. *32*

DATE		ITEM	POST. REF.	DEBIT	CREDIT	BALANCE	
						DEBIT	CREDIT

PROBLEM 4-6 ___, Continued

ACCOUNT *Income Summary* ACCOUNT NO. 33

DATE		ITEM	POST. REF.	DEBIT	CREDIT	BALANCE	
						DEBIT	CREDIT

ACCOUNT *Fees Earned* ACCOUNT NO. 41

DATE		ITEM	POST. REF.	DEBIT	CREDIT	BALANCE	
						DEBIT	CREDIT

ACCOUNT *Salary Expense* ACCOUNT NO. 51

DATE		ITEM	POST. REF.	DEBIT	CREDIT	BALANCE	
						DEBIT	CREDIT

ACCOUNT *Rent Expense* ACCOUNT NO. 52

DATE		ITEM	POST. REF.	DEBIT	CREDIT	BALANCE	
						DEBIT	CREDIT

PROBLEM 4-6 ___, Continued

ACCOUNT *Supplies Expense* ACCOUNT NO. 53

DATE		ITEM	POST. REF.	DEBIT	CREDIT	BALANCE	
						DEBIT	CREDIT

ACCOUNT *Depreciation Expense* ACCOUNT NO. 54

DATE		ITEM	POST. REF.	DEBIT	CREDIT	BALANCE	
						DEBIT	CREDIT

ACCOUNT *Insurance Expense* ACCOUNT NO. 55

DATE		ITEM	POST. REF.	DEBIT	CREDIT	BALANCE	
						DEBIT	CREDIT

ACCOUNT *Miscellaneous Expense* ACCOUNT NO. 59

DATE		ITEM	POST. REF.	DEBIT	CREDIT	BALANCE	
						DEBIT	CREDIT

PROBLEM 4-6 ___, Continued

3.

Unadjusted Trial Balance

Name ______________________________

PROBLEM 4-6 ___, Continued

6.

JOURNAL

PAGE 3

	DATE		DESCRIPTION	POST. REF.	DEBIT	CREDIT	
1			*Adjusting Entries*				1
2							2
3							3
4							4
5							5
6							6
7							7
8							8
9							9
10							10
11							11
12							12
13							13
14							14
15							15
16							16
17							17
18							18
19							19
20							20
21							21
22							22
23							23
24							24
25							25
26							26
27							27
28							28
29							29
30							30
31							31
32							32
33							33
34							34
35							35
36							36

PROBLEM 4-6 ___, Continued

7.

Adjusted Trial Balance

PROBLEM 4-6 ___, Continued

8.

Income Statement

Statement of Owner's Equity

Name ____________________

PROBLEM 4-6 ___, Continued

Balance Sheet

Name ____________________

PROBLEM 4-6 ___, Continued

5. Optional (Appendix)

	A	B	C	D	E	F	G	H	I	J	K
1											
2			End-of-Period Spreadsheet (Work Sheet)								
3											
4		Unadjusted				Adjusted		Income		Balance	
5		Trial Balance		Adjustments		Trial Balance		Statement		Sheet	
6	Account Title	Dr.	Cr.	Dr.	Cr.	Dr.	Cr.	Dr.	Cr.	Dr.	Cr.
7											
8											
9											
10											
11											
12											
13											
14											
15											
16											
17											
18											
19											
20											
21											
22											
23											
24											
25											
26											
27											
28											
29											
30											
31											
32											

PROBLEM 4-6 ___, Concluded

9. **JOURNAL** PAGE *4*

	DATE		DESCRIPTION	POST. REF.	DEBIT	CREDIT	
1			*Closing Entries*				1
2							2
3							3
4							4
5							5
6							6
7							7
8							8
9							9
10							10
11							11
12							12
13							13
14							14
15							15
16							16
17							17
18							18

10.

Post-Closing Trial Balance

Name ____________________

CONTINUING PROBLEM

1. Optional (Appendix)

	A	B	C	D	E	F	G	H	I	J	K
1											
2			End-of-Period Spreadsheet (Work Sheet)								
3											
4		Unadjusted				Adjusted		Income		Balance	
5		Trial Balance		Adjustments		Trial Balance		Statement		Sheet	
6	Account Title	Dr.	Cr.	Dr.	Cr.	Dr.	Cr.	Dr.	Cr.	Dr.	Cr.
7											
8											
9											
10											
11											
12											
13											
14											
15											
16											
17											
18											
19											
20											
21											
22											
23											
24											
25											
26											
27											
28											
29											
30											
31											
32											

CONTINUING PROBLEM, Continued

2.

Income Statement

Statement of Owner's Equity

Name ______________________________

CONTINUING PROBLEM, Continued

Balance Sheet

CONTINUING PROBLEM, Continued

3. Note: Use the general ledger accounts provided in Chapter 3, page 116–121.

JOURNAL

PAGE *4*

	DATE		DESCRIPTION	POST. REF.	DEBIT	CREDIT	
1			*Closing Entries*				1
2							2
3							3
4							4
5							5
6							6
7							7
8							8
9							9
10							10
11							11
12							12
13							13
14							14
15							15
16							16
17							17
18							18
19							19
20							20
21							21
22							22
23							23
24							24
25							25
26							26
27							27
28							28
29							29
30							30
31							31
32							32
33							33
34							34

Name ______________________________

CONTINUING PROBLEM, Concluded

4.

Post-Closing Trial Balance

COMPREHENSIVE PROBLEM 1

1. and 2.

JOURNAL

PAGE 5

DATE		DESCRIPTION	POST. REF.	DEBIT	CREDIT

COMPREHENSIVE PROBLEM 1, Continued

JOURNAL

PAGE 6

	DATE		DESCRIPTION	POST. REF.	DEBIT	CREDIT	
1							1
2							2
3							3
4							4
5							5
6							6
7							7
8							8
9							9
10							10
11							11
12							12
13							13
14							14
15							15
16							16
17							17
18							18
19							19
20							20
21							21
22							22
23							23
24							24
25							25
26							26
27							27
28							28
29							29
30							30
31							31
32							32
33							33
34							34
35							35

Name ______________________________

COMPREHENSIVE PROBLEM 1, Continued

1., 2., 6., and 9.

ACCOUNT *Cash* ACCOUNT NO. *11*

DATE		ITEM	POST. REF.	DEBIT	CREDIT	BALANCE DEBIT	BALANCE CREDIT

ACCOUNT *Accounts Receivable* ACCOUNT NO. *12*

DATE		ITEM	POST. REF.	DEBIT	CREDIT	BALANCE DEBIT	BALANCE CREDIT

ACCOUNT *Supplies* ACCOUNT NO. *14*

DATE		ITEM	POST. REF.	DEBIT	CREDIT	BALANCE DEBIT	BALANCE CREDIT

COMPREHENSIVE PROBLEM 1, Continued

ACCOUNT *Prepaid Rent* ACCOUNT NO. *15*

DATE		ITEM	POST. REF.	DEBIT	CREDIT	BALANCE DEBIT	BALANCE CREDIT

ACCOUNT *Prepaid Insurance* ACCOUNT NO. *16*

DATE		ITEM	POST. REF.	DEBIT	CREDIT	BALANCE DEBIT	BALANCE CREDIT

ACCOUNT *Office Equipment* ACCOUNT NO. *18*

DATE		ITEM	POST. REF.	DEBIT	CREDIT	BALANCE DEBIT	BALANCE CREDIT

ACCOUNT *Accumulated Depreciation* ACCOUNT NO. *19*

DATE		ITEM	POST. REF.	DEBIT	CREDIT	BALANCE DEBIT	BALANCE CREDIT

ACCOUNT *Accounts Payable* ACCOUNT NO. *21*

DATE		ITEM	POST. REF.	DEBIT	CREDIT	BALANCE DEBIT	BALANCE CREDIT

Name ______________________________

COMPREHENSIVE PROBLEM 1, Continued

ACCOUNT *Salaries Payable* ACCOUNT NO. *22*

DATE		ITEM	POST. REF.	DEBIT	CREDIT	BALANCE DEBIT	BALANCE CREDIT

ACCOUNT *Unearned Fees* ACCOUNT NO. *23*

DATE		ITEM	POST. REF.	DEBIT	CREDIT	BALANCE DEBIT	BALANCE CREDIT

ACCOUNT *Kelly Pitney, Capital* ACCOUNT NO. *31*

DATE		ITEM	POST. REF.	DEBIT	CREDIT	BALANCE DEBIT	BALANCE CREDIT

ACCOUNT *Kelly Pitney, Drawing* ACCOUNT NO. *32*

DATE		ITEM	POST. REF.	DEBIT	CREDIT	BALANCE DEBIT	BALANCE CREDIT

COMPREHENSIVE PROBLEM 1, Continued

ACCOUNT *Income Summary* ACCOUNT NO. *33*

DATE		ITEM	POST. REF.	DEBIT	CREDIT	BALANCE	
						DEBIT	CREDIT

ACCOUNT *Fees Earned* ACCOUNT NO. *41*

DATE		ITEM	POST. REF.	DEBIT	CREDIT	BALANCE	
						DEBIT	CREDIT

ACCOUNT *Salary Expense* ACCOUNT NO. *51*

DATE		ITEM	POST. REF.	DEBIT	CREDIT	BALANCE	
						DEBIT	CREDIT

ACCOUNT *Rent Expense* ACCOUNT NO. *52*

DATE		ITEM	POST. REF.	DEBIT	CREDIT	BALANCE	
						DEBIT	CREDIT

COMPREHENSIVE PROBLEM 1, Continued

ACCOUNT *Supplies Expense* ACCOUNT NO. *53*

DATE		ITEM	POST. REF.	DEBIT	CREDIT	BALANCE DEBIT	BALANCE CREDIT

ACCOUNT *Depreciation Expense* ACCOUNT NO. *54*

DATE		ITEM	POST. REF.	DEBIT	CREDIT	BALANCE DEBIT	BALANCE CREDIT

ACCOUNT *Insurance Expense* ACCOUNT NO. *55*

DATE		ITEM	POST. REF.	DEBIT	CREDIT	BALANCE DEBIT	BALANCE CREDIT

ACCOUNT *Miscellaneous Expense* ACCOUNT NO. *59*

DATE		ITEM	POST. REF.	DEBIT	CREDIT	BALANCE DEBIT	BALANCE CREDIT

COMPREHENSIVE PROBLEM 1, Continued

3.

Unadjusted Trial Balance

Name ______________________

COMPREHENSIVE PROBLEM 1, Continued

5.Optional (Appendix)

	A	B	C	D	E	F	G	H	I	J	K
1											
2			End-of-Period Spreadsheet (Work Sheet)								
3											
4		Unadjusted				Adjusted		Income		Balance	
5		Trial Balance		Adjustments		Trial Balance		Statement		Sheet	
6	Account Title	Dr.	Cr.	Dr.	Cr.	Dr.	Cr.	Dr.	Cr.	Dr.	Cr.
7											
8											
9											
10											
11											
12											
13											
14											
15											
16											
17											
18											
19											
20											
21											
22											
23											
24											
25											
26											
27											
28											
29											
30											
31											
32											

COMPREHENSIVE PROBLEM 1, Continued

6.

JOURNAL

PAGE *7*

	DATE		DESCRIPTION	POST. REF.	DEBIT	CREDIT	
1			*Adjusting Entries*				1
2							2
3							3
4							4
5							5
6							6
7							7
8							8
9							9
10							10
11							11
12							12
13							13
14							14
15							15
16							16
17							17
18							18
19							19
20							20
21							21
22							22
23							23
24							24
25							25
26							26
27							27
28							28
29							29
30							30
31							31
32							32
33							33
34							34

COMPREHENSIVE PROBLEM 1, Continued

7.

Adjusted Trial Balance

COMPREHENSIVE PROBLEM 1, Continued

8.

Income Statement

Statement of Owner's Equity

Name ____________________

COMPREHENSIVE PROBLEM 1, Continued

Balance Sheet

COMPREHENSIVE PROBLEM 1, Continued

9.

JOURNAL

PAGE *8*

DATE		DESCRIPTION	POST. REF.	DEBIT	CREDIT
		Closing Entries			

COMPREHENSIVE PROBLEM 1, Concluded

10.

Post-Closing Trial Balance

EXERCISE 5-1

REVENUE JOURNAL

Date	Invoice No.	Account Debited	Post. Ref.	Accounts Rec. Dr. Fees Earned Cr.
2010				
Nov. 1	112	Environmental Safety Co.	(a) ________	$2,625
10	113	Jenkins Co.	(b) ________	1,050
18	114	Eco-Systems	(c) ________	1,600
27	115	TEK Corp.	(d) ________	965
30				$6,240
				(e) ________

EXERCISE 5-2

a., b., and c.

GENERAL LEDGER

ACCOUNTS RECEIVABLE SUBSIDIARY LEDGER

EXERCISE 5-2, Concluded

d.

Account Receivable Subsidiary Ledger

EXERCISE 5-3

a. ______________________________

b. ______________________________

c. ______________________________

d. ______________________________

e. ______________________________

f. ______________________________

g. ______________________________

h. ______________________________

i. ______________________________

j. ______________________________

EXERCISE 5-4

a. ______________________________

b. ______________________________

c. ______________________________

d. ______________________________

e. ______________________________

f. ______________________________

g. ______________________________

h. ______________________________

i. ______________________________

j. ______________________________

k. ______________________________

EXERCISE 5-5

Nov. 3 ______________________

____

____

Nov. 6 ______________________

____

____

Nov. 13 ______________________

____

____

EXERCISE 5-6

a.

REVENUE JOURNAL PAGE

	DATE		INVOICE NO.	ACCOUNT DEBITED	POST. REF.	ACCTS. REC. DR. FEES EARNED CR.	
1							1
2							2
3							3
4							4
5							5
6							6
7							7
8							8
9							9
10							10
11							11
12							12
13							13
14							14
15							15

b. ______________________

____

____

c. ______________________

EXERCISE 5-7

a. and b.

Accounts Receivable—Arnott Co.

Accounts Receivable—Brown Co.

Accounts Receivable—Life Star Inc.

c.

Accounts Receivable—Control

Fees Earned

d.

Accounts Receivable Subsidiary Ledger

Name ______________________________

EXERCISE 5-8

Accounts Receivable Subsidiary Ledger

Accounts Receivable
(Control)

EXERCISE 5-9

REVENUE JOURNAL

PAGE 8

	DATE		INVOICE NO.	ACCOUNT DEBITED	POST. REF.	ACCTS. REC. DR. FEES EARNED CR.	
1							1
2							2
3							3
4							4
5							5
6							6
7							7
8							8
9							9
10							10
11							11
12							12
13							13
14							14
15							15

CASH RECEIPTS JOURNAL

PAGE 12

	DATE		ACCOUNT CREDITED	POST. REF.	FEES EARNED CR.	ACCOUNTS REC. CR.	CASH DR.	
1								1
2								2
3								3
4								4
5								5
6								6
7								7
8								8
9								9
10								10
11								11
12								12
13								13
14								14
15								15

EXERCISE 5-10

a.

REVENUE JOURNAL

PAGE *19*

	DATE	INVOICE NO.	ACCOUNT DEBITED	POST. REF.	ACCTS. REC. DR. FEES EARNED CR.	
1						1
2						2
3						3
4						4
5						5
6						6
7						7
8						8
9						9
10						10
11						11
12						12
13						13
14						14
15						15

CASH RECEIPTS JOURNAL

PAGE *25*

	DATE	ACCOUNT CREDITED	POST. REF.	FEES EARNED CR.	ACCOUNTS REC. CR.	CASH DR.	
1							1
2							2
3							3
4							4
5							5
6							6
7							7
8							8
9							9
10							10
11							11
12							12
13							13
14							14
15							15

EXERCISE 5-10, Concluded

b.

Accounts Receivable Subsidiary Ledger

Accounts Receivable—Control

EXERCISE 5-11

a. ____________________

b. ____________________

c. ____________________

d. ____________________

e. ____________________

f. ____________________

g. ____________________

h. ____________________

i. ____________________

j. ____________________

k. ____________________

l. ____________________

m. ____________________

Name ______________________________

EXERCISE 5-12

a. ______________________________

b. ______________________________

c. ______________________________

d. ______________________________

e. ______________________________

f. ______________________________

g. ______________________________

h. ______________________________

i. ______________________________

j. ______________________________

k. ______________________________

l. ______________________________

EXERCISE 5-13

Oct. 6 ______________________________

____

Oct. 11 ______________________________

____

Oct. 16 ______________________________

____

EXERCISE 5-14

PURCHASES JOURNAL

	DATE	ACCOUNT CREDITED	POST. REF.	ACCOUNTS PAYABLE CR.	OFFICE SUPPLIES DR.	OTHER ACCOUNTS DR.			
						ACCOUNT	POST. REF.	AMOUNT	
1									1
2									2
3									3
4									4
5									5
6									6
7									7
8									8
9									9

b. ____

____

c. ____

EXERCISE 5-15

a. and b.

Accounts Payable—Crystal Cleaning Supplies Inc.

Accounts Payable—Lawson Co.

Accounts Payable—Office Mate Inc.

c.

Accounts Payable—Control

Cleaning Supplies

d.

Accounts Payable Subsidiary Ledger

EXERCISE 5-16

Accounts Payable Subsidiary Ledger

Accounts Payable

(Control)

Name ______________________

EXERCISE 5-17

PURCHASES JOURNAL

PAGE *36*

	DATE	ACCOUNT CREDITED	POST. REF.	ACCOUNTS PAYABLE CR.	CLEANING SUPPLIES DR.	OTHER ACCOUNTS DR. ACCOUNT	OTHER ACCOUNTS DR. POST. REF.	OTHER ACCOUNTS DR. AMOUNT	
1									1
2									2
3									3
4									4
5									5
6									6
7									7
8									8
9									9

CASH PAYMENTS JOURNAL

PAGE *41*

	DATE	CK. NO.	ACCOUNT DEBITED	POST. REF.	OTHER ACCOUNTS DR.	ACCOUNTS PAYABLE DR.	CASH CR.	
1								1
2								2
3								3
4								4
5								5
6								6
7								7
8								8
9								9

Name ____________________

EXERCISE 5-18

a.

PURCHASES JOURNAL

PAGE *16*

	DATE		ACCOUNT CREDITED	POST. REF.	ACCOUNTS PAYABLE CR.	PET SUPPLIES DR.	OTHER ACCOUNTS DR.			
							ACCOUNT	POST. REF.	AMOUNT	
1										1
2										2
3										3
4										4
5										5
6										6
7										7
8										8
9										9

CASH PAYMENTS JOURNAL

PAGE *22*

	DATE		CK. NO.	ACCOUNT DEBITED	POST. REF.	OTHER ACCOUNTS DR.	ACCOUNTS PAYABLE DR.	CASH CR.	
1									1
2									2
3									3
4									4
5									5
6									6
7									7
8									8
9									9

Name ______________________________

EXERCISE 5-18, Concluded

b.

Accounts Payable Subsidiary Ledger

Accounts Payable—Control

EXERCISE 5-19

a.

EXERCISE 5-19, Concluded

b.

Accounts Payable Subsidiary Ledger

EXERCISE 5-20

Revenue journal: ______________________

Cash receipts journal: ______________________

Purchases journal: ______________________

Cash payments journal: ______________________

General journal: ______________________

EXERCISE 5-21

EXERCISE 5-22

a.

REVENUE JOURNAL

PAGE *1*

	DATE		INV. NO.	ACCOUNT DEBITED	POST. REF.	ACCOUNTS REC. DR.	FEES EARNED CR.	SALES TAX PAYABLE CR.	
1									1
2									2
3									3
4									4
5									5
6									6
7									7
8									8
9									9
10									10
11									11

JOURNAL

PAGE *1*

	DATE		DESCRIPTION	POST. REF.	DEBIT	CREDIT	
1							1
2							2
3							3
4							4
5							5
6							6
7							7

EXERCISE 5-22, Continued

ACCOUNTS RECEIVABLE SUBSIDIARY LEDGER

NAME

DATE		ITEM	POST. REF.	DEBIT	CREDIT	BALANCE

NAME

DATE		ITEM	POST. REF.	DEBIT	CREDIT	BALANCE

NAME

DATE		ITEM	POST. REF.	DEBIT	CREDIT	BALANCE

NAME

DATE		ITEM	POST. REF.	DEBIT	CREDIT	BALANCE

EXERCISE 5-22, Concluded

GENERAL LEDGER

b.

ACCOUNT *Accounts Receivable* ACCOUNT NO. *12*

DATE		ITEM	POST. REF.	DEBIT	CREDIT	BALANCE DEBIT	BALANCE CREDIT

ACCOUNT *Office Supplies* ACCOUNT NO. *14*

DATE		ITEM	POST. REF.	DEBIT	CREDIT	BALANCE DEBIT	BALANCE CREDIT

ACCOUNT *Sales Tax Payable* ACCOUNT NO. *22*

DATE		ITEM	POST. REF.	DEBIT	CREDIT	BALANCE DEBIT	BALANCE CREDIT

ACCOUNT *Fees Earned* ACCOUNT NO. *41*

DATE		ITEM	POST. REF.	DEBIT	CREDIT	BALANCE DEBIT	BALANCE CREDIT

c. 1. ______________________

2. ______________________

EXERCISE 5-23

a.–c.

EXERCISE 5-24

a.

Amazon.com:

b.

Dell Inc.:

c.

W.W. Grainger, Inc.:

d.

L.L. Bean, Inc.:

e.

Smurfit-Stone Container Corporation:

f.

Intuit Inc.:

EXERCISE 5-25

a.

	2007 (in millions)	2006 (in millions)	Increase (Decrease)	
			Amount	Percent

b.

	2007		2006	
	Amount	Percent	Amount	Percent

EXERCISE 5-25, Concluded

c.

EXERCISE 5-26

a.

Major Product Segments	Fiscal Year 2006 (in millions)	Percent

c.

Name ______________________________

PROBLEM 5-1 ___

1. and 2.

REVENUE JOURNAL

PAGE *1*

	DATE		INVOICE NO.	ACCOUNT DEBITED	POST. REF.	ACCTS. REC. DR. FEES EARNED CR.	
1							1
2							2
3							3
4							4
5							5
6							6
7							7
8							8
9							9
10							10
11							11

JOURNAL

PAGE *1*

	DATE		DESCRIPTION	POST. REF.	DEBIT	CREDIT	
1							1
2							2
3							3
4							4
5							5
6							6

PROBLEM 5-1 ___, Continued

GENERAL LEDGER

2.

ACCOUNT ACCOUNT NO.

DATE		ITEM	POST. REF.	DEBIT	CREDIT	BALANCE DEBIT	BALANCE CREDIT

ACCOUNT ACCOUNT NO.

DATE		ITEM	POST. REF.	DEBIT	CREDIT	BALANCE DEBIT	BALANCE CREDIT

ACCOUNT ACCOUNT NO.

DATE		ITEM	POST. REF.	DEBIT	CREDIT	BALANCE DEBIT	BALANCE CREDIT

ACCOUNTS RECEIVABLE LEDGER

1.

NAME

DATE		ITEM	POST. REF.	DEBIT	CREDIT	BALANCE

PROBLEM 5-1 ___, Concluded

NAME

DATE		ITEM	POST. REF.	DEBIT	CREDIT	BALANCE

NAME

DATE		ITEM	POST. REF.	DEBIT	CREDIT	BALANCE

NAME

DATE		ITEM	POST. REF.	DEBIT	CREDIT	BALANCE

NAME

DATE		ITEM	POST. REF.	DEBIT	CREDIT	BALANCE

3. a. ______________________

b. ______________________

4.

____

____

____

PROBLEM 5-2 ___

GENERAL LEDGER

1. and 5.

ACCOUNT ACCOUNT NO.

DATE		ITEM	POST. REF.	DEBIT	CREDIT	BALANCE	
						DEBIT	CREDIT

ACCOUNT ACCOUNT NO.

DATE		ITEM	POST. REF.	DEBIT	CREDIT	BALANCE	
						DEBIT	CREDIT

ACCOUNT ACCOUNT NO.

DATE		ITEM	POST. REF.	DEBIT	CREDIT	BALANCE	
						DEBIT	CREDIT

ACCOUNT ACCOUNT NO.

DATE		ITEM	POST. REF.	DEBIT	CREDIT	BALANCE	
						DEBIT	CREDIT

PROBLEM 5-2 ___, Continued

ACCOUNTS RECEIVABLE SUBSIDIARY LEDGER

2. and 4.

NAME

DATE		ITEM	POST. REF.	DEBIT	CREDIT	BALANCE

NAME

DATE		ITEM	POST. REF.	DEBIT	CREDIT	BALANCE

NAME

DATE		ITEM	POST. REF.	DEBIT	CREDIT	BALANCE

NAME

DATE		ITEM	POST. REF.	DEBIT	CREDIT	BALANCE

PROBLEM 5-2 __, Continued

3., 4., and 5.

REVENUE JOURNAL

PAGE *40*

	DATE		INVOICE NO.	ACCOUNT DEBITED	POST. REF.	ACCTS. REC. DR. FEES EARNED CR.	
1							1
2							2
3							3
4							4
5							5
6							6
7							7
8							8
9							9
10							10
11							11
12							12
13							13
14							14
15							15

JOURNAL

PAGE *1*

	DATE		DESCRIPTION	POST. REF.	DEBIT	CREDIT	
1							1
2							2
3							3
4							4
5							5
6							6
7							7
8							8
9							9
10							10

PROBLEM 5-2 ___, Concluded

CASH RECEIPTS JOURNAL

PAGE *36*

	DATE		ACCOUNT CREDITED	POST. REF.	FEES EARNED CR.	ACCOUNTS REC. CR.	CASH DR.	
1								1
2								2
3								3
4								4
5								5
6								6
7								7
8								8
9								9
10								10
11								11
12								12
13								13
14								14
15								15
16								16
17								17
18								18
19								19

6. ____

____

____

PROBLEM 5-3 ___

GENERAL LEDGER

1. and 4.

ACCOUNT *Field Supplies* ACCOUNT NO. *14*

DATE		ITEM	POST. REF.	DEBIT	CREDIT	BALANCE	
						DEBIT	CREDIT

ACCOUNT *Office Supplies* ACCOUNT NO. *15*

DATE		ITEM	POST. REF.	DEBIT	CREDIT	BALANCE	
						DEBIT	CREDIT

ACCOUNT *Office Equipment* ACCOUNT NO. *18*

DATE		ITEM	POST. REF.	DEBIT	CREDIT	BALANCE	
						DEBIT	CREDIT

ACCOUNT *Accounts Payable* ACCOUNT NO. *21*

DATE		ITEM	POST. REF.	DEBIT	CREDIT	BALANCE	
						DEBIT	CREDIT

PROBLEM 5-3 ___, Continued

ACCOUNTS PAYABLE SUBSIDIARY LEDGER

2. and 3.

NAME

DATE		ITEM	POST. REF.	DEBIT	CREDIT	BALANCE

NAME

DATE		ITEM	POST. REF.	DEBIT	CREDIT	BALANCE

NAME

DATE		ITEM	POST. REF.	DEBIT	CREDIT	BALANCE

NAME

DATE		ITEM	POST. REF.	DEBIT	CREDIT	BALANCE

NAME

DATE		ITEM	POST. REF.	DEBIT	CREDIT	BALANCE

5. a. ____________________

b. ____________________

Name ____________________ *Chapter 5*

PROBLEM 5-3 ___, Concluded

3. and 4.

PURCHASES JOURNAL

PAGE *30*

	DATE		ACCOUNT CREDITED	POST. REF.	ACCOUNTS PAYABLE CR.	FIELD SUPPLIES DR.	OFFICE SUPPLIES DR.	OTHER ACCOUNTS DR.			
								ACCOUNT	POST. REF.	AMOUNT	
1											1
2											2
3											3
4											4
5											5
6											6
7											7
8											8
9											9
10											10
11											11
12											12
13											13
14											14
15											15
16											16
17											17
18											18
19											19
20											20
21											21
22											22
23											23

Name ____________________

PROBLEM 5-4 ___

1., 2., and 3.

PURCHASES JOURNAL

PAGE *1*

	DATE	ACCOUNT CREDITED	POST. REF.	ACCOUNTS PAYABLE CR.	FIELD SUPPLIES DR.	OFFICE SUPPLIES DR.	OTHER ACCOUNTS DR.			
							ACCOUNT	POST. REF.	AMOUNT	
1										1
2										2
3										3
4										4
5										5
6										6
7										7
8										8
9										9
10										10
11										11
12										12
13										13
14										14
15										15
16										16
17										17
18										18
19										19
20										20
21										21
22										22
23										23

PROBLEM 5-4 ___, Continued

1., 2., and 3.

CASH PAYMENTS JOURNAL

PAGE 1

	DATE		CK. NO.	ACCOUNT DEBITED	POST. REF.	OTHER ACCOUNTS DR.	ACCOUNTS PAYABLE DR.	CASH CR.	
1									1
2									2
3									3
4									4
5									5
6									6
7									7
8									8
9									9
10									10
11									11
12									12
13									13
14									14
15									15
16									16
17									17

1. and 2.

JOURNAL

PAGE 1

	DATE		DESCRIPTION	POST. REF.	DEBIT	CREDIT	
1							1
2							2
3							3
4							4
5							5
6							6
7							7
8							8
9							9
10							10
11							11
12							12

PROBLEM 5-4 ___, Continued

ACCOUNTS PAYABLE LEDGER

1.

NAME ________________________________

DATE		ITEM	POST. REF.	DEBIT	CREDIT	BALANCE

NAME ________________________________

DATE		ITEM	POST. REF.	DEBIT	CREDIT	BALANCE

NAME ________________________________

DATE		ITEM	POST. REF.	DEBIT	CREDIT	BALANCE

PROBLEM 5-4 ___, Continued

GENERAL LEDGER

2. and 3.

ACCOUNT ACCOUNT NO.

DATE		ITEM	POST. REF.	DEBIT	CREDIT	BALANCE	
						DEBIT	CREDIT

ACCOUNT ACCOUNT NO.

DATE		ITEM	POST. REF.	DEBIT	CREDIT	BALANCE	
						DEBIT	CREDIT

ACCOUNT ACCOUNT NO.

DATE		ITEM	POST. REF.	DEBIT	CREDIT	BALANCE	
						DEBIT	CREDIT

ACCOUNT ACCOUNT NO.

DATE		ITEM	POST. REF.	DEBIT	CREDIT	BALANCE	
						DEBIT	CREDIT

ACCOUNT ACCOUNT NO.

DATE		ITEM	POST. REF.	DEBIT	CREDIT	BALANCE	
						DEBIT	CREDIT

PROBLEM 5-4 ___, Continued

ACCOUNT ACCOUNT NO.

DATE		ITEM	POST. REF.	DEBIT	CREDIT	BALANCE	
						DEBIT	CREDIT

ACCOUNT ACCOUNT NO.

DATE		ITEM	POST. REF.	DEBIT	CREDIT	BALANCE	
						DEBIT	CREDIT

ACCOUNT ACCOUNT NO.

DATE		ITEM	POST. REF.	DEBIT	CREDIT	BALANCE	
						DEBIT	CREDIT

ACCOUNT ACCOUNT NO.

DATE		ITEM	POST. REF.	DEBIT	CREDIT	BALANCE	
						DEBIT	CREDIT

ACCOUNT ACCOUNT NO.

DATE		ITEM	POST. REF.	DEBIT	CREDIT	BALANCE	
						DEBIT	CREDIT

PROBLEM 5-4 ___, Concluded

4.

Accounts Payable Subsidiary Ledger

PROBLEM 5-5 ___

GENERAL LEDGER

1., 3., and 4.

ACCOUNT *Cash* ACCOUNT NO. *11*

DATE		ITEM	POST. REF.	DEBIT	CREDIT	BALANCE DEBIT	BALANCE CREDIT

ACCOUNT *Accounts Receivable* ACCOUNT NO. *12*

DATE		ITEM	POST. REF.	DEBIT	CREDIT	BALANCE DEBIT	BALANCE CREDIT

ACCOUNT *Maintenance Supplies* ACCOUNT NO. *14*

DATE		ITEM	POST. REF.	DEBIT	CREDIT	BALANCE DEBIT	BALANCE CREDIT

ACCOUNT *Office Supplies* ACCOUNT NO. *15*

DATE		ITEM	POST. REF.	DEBIT	CREDIT	BALANCE DEBIT	BALANCE CREDIT

PROBLEM 5-5 ___, Continued

ACCOUNT *Office Equipment* ACCOUNT NO. *16*

DATE		ITEM	POST. REF.	DEBIT	CREDIT	BALANCE	
						DEBIT	CREDIT

ACCOUNT *Accumulated Depreciation—Office Equipment* ACCOUNT NO. *17*

DATE		ITEM	POST. REF.	DEBIT	CREDIT	BALANCE	
						DEBIT	CREDIT

ACCOUNT *Vehicles* ACCOUNT NO. *18*

DATE		ITEM	POST. REF.	DEBIT	CREDIT	BALANCE	
						DEBIT	CREDIT

ACCOUNT *Accumulated Depreciation—Vehicles* ACCOUNT NO. *19*

DATE		ITEM	POST. REF.	DEBIT	CREDIT	BALANCE	
						DEBIT	CREDIT

Name ________________________________

PROBLEM 5-5 ___, Continued

ACCOUNT *Accounts Payable* ACCOUNT NO. *21*

DATE		ITEM	POST. REF.	DEBIT	CREDIT	BALANCE	
						DEBIT	CREDIT

ACCOUNT ________________________, *Capital* ACCOUNT NO. *31*

DATE		ITEM	POST. REF.	DEBIT	CREDIT	BALANCE	
						DEBIT	CREDIT

ACCOUNT ________________________, *Drawing* ACCOUNT NO. *32*

DATE		ITEM	POST. REF.	DEBIT	CREDIT	BALANCE	
						DEBIT	CREDIT

ACCOUNT *Fees Earned* ACCOUNT NO. *41*

DATE		ITEM	POST. REF.	DEBIT	CREDIT	BALANCE	
						DEBIT	CREDIT

PROBLEM 5-5 ___, Continued

ACCOUNT *Rent Revenue* ACCOUNT NO. *42*

DATE		ITEM	POST. REF.	DEBIT	CREDIT	BALANCE	
						DEBIT	CREDIT

ACCOUNT *Driver Salaries Expense* ACCOUNT NO. *51*

DATE		ITEM	POST. REF.	DEBIT	CREDIT	BALANCE	
						DEBIT	CREDIT

ACCOUNT *Maintenance Supplies Expense* ACCOUNT NO. *52*

DATE		ITEM	POST. REF.	DEBIT	CREDIT	BALANCE	
						DEBIT	CREDIT

ACCOUNT *Fuel Expense* ACCOUNT NO. *53*

DATE		ITEM	POST. REF.	DEBIT	CREDIT	BALANCE	
						DEBIT	CREDIT

Name ____________________

PROBLEM 5-5 ___, Continued

ACCOUNT *Office Salaries Expense* ACCOUNT NO. *61*

DATE		ITEM	POST. REF.	DEBIT	CREDIT	BALANCE	
						DEBIT	CREDIT

ACCOUNT *Rent Expense* ACCOUNT NO. *62*

DATE		ITEM	POST. REF.	DEBIT	CREDIT	BALANCE	
						DEBIT	CREDIT

ACCOUNT *Advertising Expense* ACCOUNT NO. *63*

DATE		ITEM	POST. REF.	DEBIT	CREDIT	BALANCE	
						DEBIT	CREDIT

ACCOUNT *Miscellaneous Administrative Expense* ACCOUNT NO. *64*

DATE		ITEM	POST. REF.	DEBIT	CREDIT	BALANCE	
						DEBIT	CREDIT

Name ______________________________ *Chapter 5*

PROBLEM 5-5 ___, Continued

2., 3., and 4.

PURCHASES JOURNAL

PAGE 37

	DATE	ACCOUNT CREDITED	POST. REF.	ACCOUNTS PAYABLE CR.	MAINTENANCE SUPPLIES DR.	OFFICE SUPPLIES DR.	OTHER ACCOUNTS DR.			
							ACCOUNT	POST. REF.	AMOUNT	
1										1
2										2
3										3
4										4
5										5
6										6
7										7
8										8
9										9
10										10
11										11
12										12
13										13
14										14
15										15
16										16
17										17
18										18
19										19
20										20
21										21
22										22
23										23

Name ____________________

PROBLEM 5-5 ___, Continued

2., 3., and 4.

CASH RECEIPTS JOURNAL

PAGE 31

	DATE		ACCOUNT CREDITED	POST. REF.	OTHER ACCOUNTS CR.	ACCOUNTS REC. CR.	CASH DR.	
1								1
2								2
3								3
4								4
5								5
6								6
7								7
8								8
9								9
10								10
11								11
12								12
13								13
14								14
15								15
16								16

2. and 4.

REVENUE JOURNAL

PAGE 35

	DATE		INVOICE NO.	ACCOUNT DEBITED	POST. REF.	ACCTS. REC. DR. FEES EARNED CR.	
1							1
2							2
3							3
4							4
5							5
6							6
7							7
8							8
9							9
10							10
11							11
12							12
13							13
14							14

PROBLEM 5-5 ___, Continued

2., 3., and 4.

CASH PAYMENTS JOURNAL

PAGE 34

	DATE		CK. NO.	ACCOUNT DEBITED	POST. REF.	OTHER ACCOUNTS DR.	ACCOUNTS PAYABLE DR.	CASH CR.	
1									1
2									2
3									3
4									4
5									5
6									6
7									7
8									8
9									9
10									10
11									11
12									12
13									13
14									14
15									15
16									16
17									17
18									18
19									19

2. and 3.

JOURNAL

PAGE 1

	DATE		DESCRIPTION	POST. REF.	DEBIT	CREDIT	
1							1
2							2
3							3
4							4
5							5
6							6
7							7
8							8
9							9
10							10
11							11

PROBLEM 5-5 ___, Concluded

5.

Unadjusted Trial Balance

6. Balance of accounts receivable control account: ____________

Balance of accounts payable control account: ____________

Name ______________________________

EXERCISE 6-1

a. ______________________________

b. ______________________________

c. ______________________________

____

EXERCISE 6-2

____

EXERCISE 6-3

a. Purchases – (X + Y) = Net purchases

____

b. Net purchases + X = Cost of merchandise purchased

____

c. Merchandise inventory (beginning) + Cost of merchandise purchased = X

____

d. Merchandise available for sale – X = Cost of merchandise sold

____

EXERCISE 6-4

a. ______________________________

EXERCISE 6-4, Concluded

b. ______________________

EXERCISE 6-5

(Optional)

EXERCISE 6-6

a. Net sales: ______________________________

b. Gross profit: ______________________________

EXERCISE 6-7

1. Advertising expense: ______________________________
2. Depreciation expense on store equipment: ______________________________
3. Insurance expense on office equipment: ______________________________
4. Interest expense on notes payable: ______________________________
5. Rent expense on office building: ______________________________
6. Salaries of office personnel: ______________________________
7. Salary of sales manager: ______________________________
8. Sales supplies used: ______________________________

EXERCISE 6-8

Income Statement

EXERCISE 6-9

(Optional)

Income Statement

EXERCISE 6-10

a. ______________________

b. ______________________

c. ______________________

d. ______________________

e. ______________________

f. ______________________

g. ______________________

h. ______________________

EXERCISE 6-11

a.

____

Income Statement

____

b.

____

____

____

____

____

____

____

EXERCISE 6-12

Balance Sheet Accounts

Acct #	Account Name

Income Statement Accounts

Acct #	Account Name

Name ______________________________

EXERCISE 6-13

JOURNAL

PAGE

	DATE		DESCRIPTION	POST. REF.	DEBIT	CREDIT	
1							1
2							2
3							3
4							4
5							5
6							6
7							7
8							8
9							9
10							10
11							11
12							12
13							13
14							14
15							15
16							16
17							17
18							18
19							19
20							20
21							21
22							22
23							23
24							24
25							25
26							26
27							27
28							28
29							29
30							30
31							31
32							32
33							33
34							34
35							35
36							36

EXERCISE 6-14

EXERCISE 6-15

a.

b.

JOURNAL PAGE

	DATE		DESCRIPTION	POST. REF.	DEBIT	CREDIT	
1							1
2							2
3							3
4							4
5							5
6							6

EXERCISE 6-16

(1)

(2)

(3)

(4)

(5)

EXERCISE 6-17

a. Amount of the sale: ______________________

b. Amount debited to Accounts Receivable: ______________________

c. Amount of the discount for early payment:

d. Amount due within the discount period: ______________________

EXERCISE 6-18

a. ______________________

____

b. ______________________

EXERCISE 6-19

____

____

____

____

____

____

____

____

____

EXERCISE 6-20

(1) ______________________

____

____

(2) ______________________

____

____

(3) ______________________

____

____

(4) ______________________

____

____

EXERCISE 6-21

JOURNAL PAGE

	DATE		DESCRIPTION	POST. REF.	DEBIT	CREDIT	
1							1
2							2
3							3
4							4
5							5
6							6
7							7
8							8
9							9
10							10

EXERCISE 6-22

JOURNAL PAGE

	DATE		DESCRIPTION	POST. REF.	DEBIT	CREDIT	
1							1
2							2
3							3
4							4
5							5
6							6
7							7
8							8
9							9
10							10
11							11
12							12
13							13
14							14
15							15
16							16

Name ______________________________

EXERCISE 6-23

	Merchandise	Freight Paid by Seller		Returns and Allowances	Amount to be Paid in Full
a.	$15,000	—	FOB destination, n/30	$800	$ ______
b.	10,000	$400	FOB shipping point, 2/10, n/30	1,200	$ ______
c.	$8,250	—	FOB shipping point, 1/10, n/30	$750	$ ______
d.	2,900	125	FOB shipping point, 2/10, n/30	400	$ ______
e.	3,850	—	FOB destination, 2/10, n/30	—	$ ______

EXERCISE 6-24

a. ______________________________

b. ______________________________

c. ______________________________

d. ______________________________

EXERCISE 6-25

JOURNAL PAGE

	DATE		DESCRIPTION	POST. REF.	DEBIT	CREDIT	
1							1
2							2
3							3
4							4
5							5
6							6
7							7
8							8
9							9
10							10
11							11
12							12

EXERCISE 6-26

JOURNAL PAGE

	DATE		DESCRIPTION	POST. REF.	DEBIT	CREDIT	
1							1
2							2
3							3
4							4
5							5
6							6
7							7
8							8
9							9
10							10
11							11
12							12
13							13
14							14
15							15
16							16
17							17
18							18

EXERCISE 6-27

JOURNAL PAGE

	DATE		DESCRIPTION	POST. REF.	DEBIT	CREDIT	
1							1
2							2
3							3
4							4
5							5
6							6
7							7
8							8
9							9
10							10
11							11
12							12

EXERCISE 6-28

	Debit	Credit
a. Cost of Merchandise Sold	______	______
b. Delivery Expense	______	______
c. Merchandise Inventory	______	______
d. Sales	______	______
e. Sales Discounts	______	______
f. Sales Returns and Allowances	______	______
g. Sales Tax Payable	______	______

EXERCISE 6-29

JOURNAL PAGE

	DATE		DESCRIPTION	POST. REF.	DEBIT	CREDIT	
1							1
2							2
3							3
4							4
5							5
6							6

EXERCISE 6-30

a. Accounts Payable: ______________________________

b. Advertising Expense: ______________________________

c. Cost of Merchandise Sold: ______________________________

d. Merchandise Inventory: ______________________________

e. Sales: ______________________________

f. Sales Discounts: ______________________________

g. Sales Returns and Allowances: ______________________________

h. Supplies: ______________________________

i. Supplies Expense: ______________________________

j. Talia Greenly, Drawing: ______________________________

k. Wages Payable: ______________________________

EXERCISE 6-31

JOURNAL

PAGE

DATE		DESCRIPTION	POST. REF.	DEBIT	CREDIT

EXERCISE 6-32

JOURNAL

PAGE

	DATE		DESCRIPTION	POST. REF.	DEBIT	CREDIT	
1							1
2							2
3							3
4							4
5							5
6							6
7							7
8							8
9							9
10							10
11							11
12							12
13							13
14							14
15							15
16							16
17							17

Name ______________________________

APPENDIX 1—EXERCISE 6-33

a. and c.

SALES JOURNAL

PAGE

	DATE	INVOICE NO.	ACCOUNT DEBITED	POST. REF.	ACCOUNTS RECEIVABLE DR. SALES CR.	COST OF MERCHANDISE SOLD DR. MERCHANDISE INVENTORY CR.	
1							1
2							2
3							3
4							4
5							5
6							6
7							7
8							8

b. and c.

PURCHASES JOURNAL

PAGE

	DATE	ACCOUNT CREDITED	POST. REF.	ACCOUNTS PAYABLE CR.	MERCHANDISE INVENTORY DR.	OTHER ACCOUNTS DR.			
						ACCOUNT	POST. REF.	AMOUNT	
1									1
2									2
3									3
4									4
5									5
6									6

APPENDIX 1—EXERCISE 6-33, Concluded

d.

APPENDIX 2—EXERCISE 6-34

1. ______________________________
2. ______________________________
3. ______________________________
4. ______________________________
5. ______________________________
6. ______________________________
7. ______________________________
8. ______________________________
9. ______________________________
10. ______________________________

APPENDIX 2—EXERCISE 6-35

a. ______________________________
b. ______________________________
c. ______________________________
d. ______________________________
e. ______________________________
f. ______________________________
g. ______________________________

APPENDIX 2—EXERCISE 6-36

JOURNAL

PAGE

	DATE		DESCRIPTION	POST. REF.	DEBIT	CREDIT	
1							1
2							2
3							3
4							4
5							5
6							6
7							7
8							8
9							9
10							10
11							11
12							12
13							13
14							14
15							15
16							16
17							17
18							18
19							19
20							20
21							21
22							22

Name ______________________________

APPENDIX 2—EXERCISE 6-37

JOURNAL

PAGE

	DATE		DESCRIPTION	POST. REF.	DEBIT	CREDIT	
1							1
2							2
3							3
4							4
5							5
6							6
7							7
8							8
9							9
10							10
11							11
12							12
13							13
14							14
15							15
16							16
17							17
18							18
19							19
20							20
21							21
22							22
23							23
24							24
25							25

APPENDIX 2—EXERCISE 6-38

JOURNAL

PAGE

DATE		DESCRIPTION	POST. REF.	DEBIT	CREDIT

EXERCISE 6-39

a. 2007: ____________________

2006: ____________________

b. ____________________

EXERCISE 6-40

a. ____________________

b. ____________________

PROBLEM 6-1 ___

1.

Income Statement

PROBLEM 6-1 ___, Continued

2.

Statement of Owner's Equity

PROBLEM 6-1 ___, Continued

3.

Balance Sheet

PROBLEM 6-1 ___, Concluded

4. a.

b.

PROBLEM 6-2 ___

1.

Income Statement

2.

Statement of Owner's Equity

PROBLEM 6-2 ___, Continued

3.

Balance Sheet

PROBLEM 6-2 ___, Concluded

4.

JOURNAL

PAGE

	DATE		DESCRIPTION	POST. REF.	DEBIT	CREDIT	
1							1
2							2
3							3
4							4
5							5
6							6
7							7
8							8
9							9
10							10
11							11
12							12
13							13
14							14
15							15
16							16
17							17
18							18
19							19
20							20
21							21
22							22
23							23
24							24
25							25
26							26
27							27
28							28
29							29
30							30
31							31
32							32
33							33
34							34
35							35
36							36

Name ________________________________

PROBLEM 6-3 ___

JOURNAL

PAGE

DATE		DESCRIPTION	POST. REF.	DEBIT	CREDIT

PROBLEM 6-3 ___, Concluded

JOURNAL

PAGE

DATE		DESCRIPTION	POST. REF.	DEBIT	CREDIT

Name ______________________________________

PROBLEM 6-4 ___

JOURNAL

PAGE

DATE		DESCRIPTION	POST. REF.	DEBIT	CREDIT

PROBLEM 6- 4___, Concluded

JOURNAL

PAGE

	DATE		DESCRIPTION	POST. REF.	DEBIT	CREDIT	
1							1
2							2
3							3
4							4
5							5
6							6
7							7
8							8
9							9
10							10
11							11
12							12
13							13
14							14
15							15
16							16
17							17
18							18
19							19
20							20
21							21
22							22
23							23
24							24
25							25
26							26
27							27
28							28
29							29
30							30
31							31
32							32
33							33
34							34
35							35
36							36

Name ______________________________

PROBLEM 6-5 ___

JOURNAL

PAGE

	DATE		DESCRIPTION	POST. REF.	DEBIT	CREDIT	
1							1
2							2
3							3
4							4
5							5
6							6
7							7
8							8
9							9
10							10
11							11
12							12
13							13
14							14
15							15
16							16
17							17
18							18
19							19
20							20
21							21
22							22
23							23
24							24
25							25
26							26
27							27
28							28
29							29
30							30
31							31
32							32
33							33
34							34
35							35
36							36

PROBLEM 6-5___, Concluded

JOURNAL

PAGE

DATE		DESCRIPTION	POST. REF.	DEBIT	CREDIT

Name ______________________________

PROBLEM 6-6 ___

1.

JOURNAL

PAGE

	DATE		DESCRIPTION	POST. REF.	DEBIT	CREDIT	
1							1
2							2
3							3
4							4
5							5
6							6
7							7
8							8
9							9
10							10
11							11
12							12
13							13
14							14
15							15
16							16
17							17
18							18
19							19
20							20
21							21
22							22
23							23
24							24
25							25
26							26
27							27
28							28
29							29
30							30
31							31
32							32
33							33
34							34
35							35
36							36

PROBLEM 6-6 ___, Concluded

2.

JOURNAL

PAGE

	DATE		DESCRIPTION	POST. REF.	DEBIT	CREDIT	
1							1
2							2
3							3
4							4
5							5
6							6
7							7
8							8
9							9
10							10
11							11
12							12
13							13
14							14
15							15
16							16
17							17
18							18
19							19
20							20
21							21
22							22
23							23
24							24
25							25
26							26
27							27
28							28
29							29
30							30
31							31
32							32
33							33
34							34
35							35
36							36

APPENDIX 2—PROBLEM 6-7 ___

JOURNAL

PAGE

DATE		DESCRIPTION	POST. REF.	DEBIT	CREDIT

APPENDIX 2—PROBLEM 6-7 ___, Concluded

JOURNAL

PAGE

DATE		DESCRIPTION	POST. REF.	DEBIT	CREDIT

APPENDIX 2—PROBLEM 6-8 ___

JOURNAL

PAGE

	DATE		DESCRIPTION	POST. REF.	DEBIT	CREDIT	
1							1
2							2
3							3
4							4
5							5
6							6
7							7
8							8
9							9
10							10
11							11
12							12
13							13
14							14
15							15
16							16
17							17
18							18
19							19
20							20
21							21
22							22
23							23
24							24
25							25
26							26
27							27
28							28
29							29
30							30
31							31
32							32
33							33
34							34
35							35
36							36

APPENDIX 2—PROBLEM 6-8 ___, Concluded

JOURNAL

PAGE

DATE		DESCRIPTION	POST. REF.	DEBIT	CREDIT

Name ______________________________

APPENDIX 2—PROBLEM 6-9 ___

1.

JOURNAL

PAGE

	DATE		DESCRIPTION	POST. REF.	DEBIT	CREDIT	
1							1
2							2
3							3
4							4
5							5
6							6
7							7
8							8
9							9
10							10
11							11
12							12
13							13
14							14
15							15
16							16
17							17
18							18
19							19
20							20
21							21
22							22
23							23
24							24
25							25
26							26
27							27
28							28
29							29
30							30
31							31
32							32
33							33
34							34
35							35
36							36

APPENDIX 2—PROBLEM 6-9 ___, Concluded

2.

JOURNAL PAGE

DATE		DESCRIPTION	POST. REF.	DEBIT	CREDIT

Name ____

APPENDIX 2—PROBLEM 6-10 ___

1.

2.

Income Statement

APPENDIX 2—PROBLEM 6-10 ___, Continued

2.

Income Statement (Continued)

APPENDIX 2—PROBLEM 6-10 ___, Concluded

3.

JOURNAL

PAGE

DATE		DESCRIPTION	POST. REF.	DEBIT	CREDIT

COMPREHENSIVE PROBLEM 2

1., 2., 6., and 9.

ACCOUNT *Cash* ACCOUNT NO. *110*

DATE		ITEM	POST. REF.	DEBIT	CREDIT	BALANCE	
						DEBIT	CREDIT

COMPREHENSIVE PROBLEM 2, Continued

ACCOUNT *Accounts Receivable* ACCOUNT NO. *112*

DATE		ITEM	POST. REF.	DEBIT	CREDIT	BALANCE	
						DEBIT	CREDIT

ACCOUNT *Merchandise Inventory* ACCOUNT NO. *115*

DATE		ITEM	POST. REF.	DEBIT	CREDIT	BALANCE	
						DEBIT	CREDIT

Name ______________________________

COMPREHENSIVE PROBLEM 2, Continued

ACCOUNT *Prepaid Insurance* ACCOUNT NO. *116*

DATE		ITEM	POST. REF.	DEBIT	CREDIT	BALANCE	
						DEBIT	CREDIT

ACCOUNT *Store Supplies* ACCOUNT NO. *117*

DATE		ITEM	POST. REF.	DEBIT	CREDIT	BALANCE	
						DEBIT	CREDIT

ACCOUNT *Store Equipment* ACCOUNT NO. *123*

DATE		ITEM	POST. REF.	DEBIT	CREDIT	BALANCE	
						DEBIT	CREDIT

ACCOUNT *Accumulated Depreciation—Store Equipment* ACCOUNT NO. *124*

DATE		ITEM	POST. REF.	DEBIT	CREDIT	BALANCE	
						DEBIT	CREDIT

COMPREHENSIVE PROBLEM 2, Continued

ACCOUNT *Accounts Payable* ACCOUNT NO. *210*

DATE		ITEM	POST. REF.	DEBIT	CREDIT	BALANCE DEBIT	BALANCE CREDIT

ACCOUNT *Salaries Payable* ACCOUNT NO. *211*

DATE		ITEM	POST. REF.	DEBIT	CREDIT	BALANCE DEBIT	BALANCE CREDIT

ACCOUNT *Rocky Hansen, Capital* ACCOUNT NO. *310*

DATE		ITEM	POST. REF.	DEBIT	CREDIT	BALANCE DEBIT	BALANCE CREDIT

ACCOUNT *Rocky Hansen, Drawing* ACCOUNT NO. *311*

DATE		ITEM	POST. REF.	DEBIT	CREDIT	BALANCE DEBIT	BALANCE CREDIT

COMPREHENSIVE PROBLEM 2, Continued

ACCOUNT *Income Summary* ACCOUNT NO. *312*

DATE		ITEM	POST. REF.	DEBIT	CREDIT	BALANCE	
						DEBIT	CREDIT

ACCOUNT *Sales* ACCOUNT NO. *410*

DATE		ITEM	POST. REF.	DEBIT	CREDIT	BALANCE	
						DEBIT	CREDIT

ACCOUNT *Sales Returns and Allowances* ACCOUNT NO. *411*

DATE		ITEM	POST. REF.	DEBIT	CREDIT	BALANCE	
						DEBIT	CREDIT

COMPREHENSIVE PROBLEM 2, Continued

ACCOUNT *Sales Discounts* ACCOUNT NO. *412*

DATE		ITEM	POST. REF.	DEBIT	CREDIT	BALANCE DEBIT	BALANCE CREDIT

ACCOUNT *Cost of Merchandise Sold* ACCOUNT NO. *510*

DATE		ITEM	POST. REF.	DEBIT	CREDIT	BALANCE DEBIT	BALANCE CREDIT

ACCOUNT *Sales Salaries Expense* ACCOUNT NO. *520*

DATE		ITEM	POST. REF.	DEBIT	CREDIT	BALANCE DEBIT	BALANCE CREDIT

Name ______________________________

COMPREHENSIVE PROBLEM 2, Continued

ACCOUNT *Advertising Expense* ACCOUNT NO. *521*

DATE		ITEM	POST. REF.	DEBIT	CREDIT	BALANCE DEBIT	BALANCE CREDIT

ACCOUNT *Depreciation Expense* ACCOUNT NO. *522*

DATE		ITEM	POST. REF.	DEBIT	CREDIT	BALANCE DEBIT	BALANCE CREDIT

ACCOUNT *Store Supplies Expense* ACCOUNT NO. *523*

DATE		ITEM	POST. REF.	DEBIT	CREDIT	BALANCE DEBIT	BALANCE CREDIT

ACCOUNT *Miscellaneous Selling Expense* ACCOUNT NO. *529*

DATE		ITEM	POST. REF.	DEBIT	CREDIT	BALANCE DEBIT	BALANCE CREDIT

COMPREHENSIVE PROBLEM 2, Continued

ACCOUNT *Office Salaries Expense* ACCOUNT NO. *530*

DATE		ITEM	POST. REF.	DEBIT	CREDIT	BALANCE DEBIT	BALANCE CREDIT

ACCOUNT *Rent Expense* ACCOUNT NO. *531*

DATE		ITEM	POST. REF.	DEBIT	CREDIT	BALANCE DEBIT	BALANCE CREDIT

ACCOUNT *Insurance Expense* ACCOUNT NO. *532*

DATE		ITEM	POST. REF.	DEBIT	CREDIT	BALANCE DEBIT	BALANCE CREDIT

ACCOUNT *Miscellaneous Administrative Expense* ACCOUNT NO. *539*

DATE		ITEM	POST. REF.	DEBIT	CREDIT	BALANCE DEBIT	BALANCE CREDIT

Name ______________________________

COMPREHENSIVE PROBLEM 2, Continued

1. and 2.

JOURNAL

PAGE 20

	DATE		DESCRIPTION	POST. REF.	DEBIT	CREDIT	
1							1
2							2
3							3
4							4
5							5
6							6
7							7
8							8
9							9
10							10
11							11
12							12
13							13
14							14
15							15
16							16
17							17
18							18
19							19
20							20
21							21
22							22
23							23
24							24
25							25
26							26
27							27
28							28
29							29
30							30
31							31
32							32
33							33
34							34
35							35
36							36

COMPREHENSIVE PROBLEM 2, Continued

JOURNAL

PAGE *20*
continued

DATE	DESCRIPTION	POST. REF.	DEBIT	CREDIT

JOURNAL

PAGE *21*

DATE	DESCRIPTION	POST. REF.	DEBIT	CREDIT

Name ______________________________

COMPREHENSIVE PROBLEM 2, Continued

JOURNAL

PAGE *21*
continued

	DATE		DESCRIPTION	POST. REF.	DEBIT	CREDIT	
1							1
2							2
3							3
4							4
5							5
6							6
7							7
8							8
9							9
10							10
11							11
12							12
13							13
14							14
15							15
16							16
17							17
18							18
19							19
20							20
21							21
22							22
23							23
24							24
25							25
26							26
27							27
28							28
29							29
30							30
31							31
32							32
33							33
34							34

COMPREHENSIVE PROBLEM 2, Continued

3.

Unadjusted Trial Balance

Name ________________________________

COMPREHENSIVE PROBLEM 2, Continued

4. and 6.

JOURNAL

PAGE *22*

DATE		DESCRIPTION	POST. REF.	DEBIT	CREDIT
		Adjusting Entries			

COMPREHENSIVE PROBLEM 2, Continued

7.

Adjusted Trial Balance

COMPREHENSIVE PROBLEM 2, Continued

8.

Income Statement

COMPREHENSIVE PROBLEM 2, Continued

Statement of Owner's Equity

COMPREHENSIVE PROBLEM 2, Continued

Balance Sheet

COMPREHENSIVE PROBLEM 2, Continued

9.

JOURNAL

PAGE 23

	DATE		DESCRIPTION	POST. REF.	DEBIT	CREDIT	
1			*Closing Entries*				1
2							2
3							3
4							4
5							5
6							6
7							7
8							8
9							9
10							10
11							11
12							12
13							13
14							14
15							15
16							16
17							17
18							18
19							19
20							20
21							21
22							22
23							23
24							24
25							25
26							26
27							27
28							28
29							29
30							30
31							31
32							32
33							33
34							34
35							35
36							36

COMPREHENSIVE PROBLEM 2, Concluded

10.

Post-Closing Trial Balance

Name ______________________

COMPREHENSIVE PROBLEM 2, Concluded

5. Optional *This work sheet is applicable only if the end-of-period spreadsheet (work sheet) is used.*

	A	B	C	D	E	F	G	H	I	J	K
1											
2			End-of-Period Spreadsheet (Work Sheet)								
3											
4		Unadjusted Trial				Adjusted Trial					
5		Balance		Adjustments		Balance		Income Statement		Balance Sheet	
6	Account Title	Dr.	Cr.	Dr.	Cr.	Dr.	Cr.	Dr.	Cr.	Dr.	Cr.
7											
8											
9											
10											
11											
12											
13											
14											
15											
16											
17											
18											
19											
20											
21											
22											
23											
24											
25											
26											
27											
28											
29											
30											
31											
32											
33											

EXERCISE 7-1

EXERCISE 7-2

a.

b.

c.

Name ______________________

EXERCISE 7-3

Portable Video CD Players									
Date	Purchases			Cost of Merchandise Sold			Inventory		
	Quantity	Unit Cost	Total Cost	Quantity	Unit Cost	Total Cost	Quantity	Unit Cost	Total Cost

Name ______________________

EXERCISE 7-4

Portable Video CD Players									
Date	Purchases			Cost of Merchandise Sold			Inventory		
	Quantity	Unit Cost	Total Cost	Quantity	Unit Cost	Total Cost	Quantity	Unit Cost	Total Cost

Name ____________________

EXERCISE 7-5

Cell Phones									
Date	Purchases			Cost of Merchandise Sold			Inventory		
	Quantity	Unit Cost	Total Cost	Quantity	Unit Cost	Total Cost	Quantity	Unit Cost	Total Cost

Name ____________________

EXERCISE 7-6

Cell Phones									
Date	Purchases			Cost of Merchandise Sold			Inventory		
	Quantity	Unit Cost	Total Cost	Quantity	Unit Cost	Total Cost	Quantity	Unit Cost	Total Cost

EXERCISE 7-7

a. FIFO: ______________________

b. LIFO: ______________________

EXERCISE 7-8

a. First-in, first-out method: ______________________

b. Last-in, first-out method: ______________________

c. Average cost method: ______________________

EXERCISE 7-9

	Cost	
Inventory Method	**Merchandise Inventory**	**Merchandise Sold**
a. First-in, first-out..............		
b. Last-in, first-out..............		
c. Average cost..................		

Supporting calculations:

EXERCISE 7-10

a. FIFO inventory __________ LIFO inventory

b. FIFO cost of goods sold __________ LIFO cost of goods sold

c. FIFO net income __________ LIFO net income

d. FIFO income tax __________ LIFO income tax

2. ______________________________

____

____

____

____

____

____

____

____

____

____

____

EXERCISE 7-11

	A	B	C	D	E	F	G
1			Unit	Unit		Total	
2		Inventory	Cost	Market			Lower
3	Commodity	Quantity	Price	Price	Cost	Market	of C or M
4	Aquarius	20	$ 80	$ 92			
5	Capricorn	50	70	65			
6	Leo	8	300	280			
7	Scorpio	30	40	30			
8	Taurus	100	90	94			
9	Total						

EXERCISE 7-12

____

____

____

____

____

EXERCISE 7-13

a. **Balance Sheet**

Merchandise inventory .... ______________

Current assets .... ______________

Total assets .... ______________

Owner's equity .... ______________

b. **Income Statement**

Cost of merchandise sold .... ______________

Gross profit .... ______________

Net income .... ______________

EXERCISE 7-14

a. **Balance Sheet**

Merchandise inventory .... ______________

Current assets .... ______________

Total assets .... ______________

Owner's equity .... ______________

b. **Income Statement**

Cost of merchandise sold .... ______________

Gross profit .... ______________

Net income .... ______________

EXERCISE 7-15

APPENDIX EXERCISE 7-16

APPENDIX EXERCISE 7-17

APPENDIX EXERCISE 7-18

APPENDIX EXERCISE 7-19

	A	B	C
1		**Cost**	**Retail**
2			
3			
4			
5			
6			
7			
8			

APPENDIX EXERCISE 7-20

a.

	A	B	C
1		Cost	Retail
2			
3			
4			
5			
6			
7			
8			

b. ________________________

APPENDIX EXERCISE 7-21

APPENDIX EXERCISE 7-22

EXERCISE 7-23

a. Apple: ____________________

American Greetings: ____________________

b. ____________________

EXERCISE 7-24

a. Number of Days' Sales in Inventory =

Kroger: ____________________

Safeway: ____________________

Winn-Dixie: ____________________

Inventory Turnover =

Kroger: ____________________

Safeway: ____________________

Winn-Dixie: ____________________

b. ____________________

EXERCISE 7-24, Concluded

c.

Name ____________________

PROBLEM 7-1 ___

1.

Date	Purchases			Cost of Merchandise Sold			Inventory		
	Quantity	Unit Cost	Total Cost	Quantity	Unit Cost	Total Cost	Quantity	Unit Cost	Total Cost

PROBLEM 7-1 ___, Concluded

2.

JOURNAL PAGE

	DATE		DESCRIPTION	POST. REF.	DEBIT	CREDIT	
1							1
2							2
3							3
4							4
5							5
6							6
7							7
8							8
9							9
10							10

3. ____

4. ____

Name ______________________________

PROBLEM 7-2 ___

1.

Date	Purchases			Cost of Merchandise Sold			Inventory		
	Quantity	Unit Cost	Total Cost	Quantity	Unit Cost	Total Cost	Quantity	Unit Cost	Total Cost

PROBLEM 7-2 ___, Concluded

2. and 3.

PROBLEM 7-3 ___

1. First-In, First-Out Method

Model	Quantity	Unit Cost	Total Cost

2. Last-In, First-Out Method

Model	Quantity	Unit Cost	Total Cost

PROBLEM 7-3 ___, Concluded

3. Average Cost Method

Model	Quantity	Unit Cost	Total Cost

Computations of unit costs:

4. a.

b.

Name ____________________

PROBLEM 7-4 ___

	A	B	C	D	E	F	G	H
1								
2	Inventory Sheet December 31, 2010							
3								
4				Unit	Unit	Total		
5		Inventory		Cost	Market			Lower
6	Description	Quantity		Price	Price	Cost	Market	of C or M
7	Alpha 10	38	30	$ 60	$ 57	$1,800	$1,710	
8			8	59		472	456	
9						2,272	2,166	$ 2,166
10	Beta 30	18			180			
11	Charlie 4	30			120			
12								
13								
14	Echo 9	125			26			
15	Frank 6	18			550			
16								
17								
18	George 15	60			15			
19	Killo 6	5			390			
20	Quebec 12	375			6			
21	Romeo 7	90			18			
22								
23								
24	Sierra 3	6			235			
25								
26								
27	Washburn 2	140			20			
28								
29								
30	X-Ray 4	15			745			
31								
32								
33	Total							
34								
35								

APPENDIX PROBLEM 7-5 ___

1.

	A	B	C
1			
2		Cost	Retail
3			
4			
5			
6			
7			
8			
9			
10			
11			
12			

2.

	A	B	C
1			
2	a.	Cost	Retail
3			
4			
5			
6			
7			
8			
9			
10			
11			
12			
13	b.		
14			
15			
16			
17			

Name ______________________________

EXERCISE 8-1

EXERCISE 8-2

a.

b.

c.

EXERCISE 8-3

a.

b.

EXERCISE 8-3, Concluded

c. ________________________

d. ________________________

EXERCISE 8-4

EXERCISE 8-5

EXERCISE 8-6

EXERCISE 8-7

EXERCISE 8-8

a.

b.

EXERCISE 8-9

a. ______________________________

b. ______________________________

EXERCISE 8-10

EXERCISE 8-11

a.

b.

EXERCISE 8-12

JOURNAL

PAGE

	DATE		DESCRIPTION	POST. REF.	DEBIT	CREDIT	
1							1
2							2
3							3
4							4
5							5
6							6
7							7
8							8
9							9
10							10
11							11
12							12
13							13
14							14

EXERCISE 8-13

JOURNAL

PAGE

	DATE		DESCRIPTION	POST. REF.	DEBIT	CREDIT	
1							1
2							2
3							3
4							4
5							5
6							6
7							7
8							8
9							9
10							10
11							11
12							12
13							13
14							14

EXERCISE 8-14

EXERCISE 8-15

EXERCISE 8-16

a. Addition to the balance per bank: ______________________

b. Deduction from the balance per bank: ______________________

c. Addition to the balance per company's records: ______________________

d. Deduction from the balance per company's records: ______________________

EXERCISE 8-17

EXERCISE 8-18

Bank Reconciliation

EXERCISE 8-19

JOURNAL PAGE

	DATE		DESCRIPTION	POST. REF.	DEBIT	CREDIT	
1							1
2							2
3							3
4							4
5							5

EXERCISE 8-20

JOURNAL PAGE

	DATE		DESCRIPTION	POST. REF.	DEBIT	CREDIT	
1							1
2							2
3							3
4							4

EXERCISE 8-21

a.

Bank Reconciliation

b. ____________________

EXERCISE 8-22

EXERCISE 8-22, Concluded

Optional

Bank Reconciliation

Name ____________________

EXERCISE 8-23

a.

b.

EXERCISE 8-24

a. and b.

JOURNAL PAGE

	DATE		DESCRIPTION	POST. REF.	DEBIT	CREDIT	
1							1
2							2
3							3
4							4
5							5
6							6
7							7
8							8

EXERCISE 8-25

EXERCISE 8-26

a.

b.

EXERCISE 8-27

a.

b.

c.

EXERCISE 8-28

a.

2006:

2005:

2004:

2003:

b.

2006:

2005:

2004:

2003:

c.

PROBLEM 8-1 ___

Name ______________________________

PROBLEM 8-2 ___

JOURNAL

PAGE

	DATE		DESCRIPTION	POST. REF.	DEBIT	CREDIT	
1							1
2							2
3							3
4							4
5							5
6							6
7							7
8							8
9							9
10							10
11							11
12							12
13							13
14							14
15							15
16							16
17							17
18							18
19							19
20							20
21							21
22							22
23							23
24							24
25							25
26							26
27							27
28							28
29							29
30							30
31							31
32							32
33							33
34							34
35							35
36							36

PROBLEM 8-3 ___

1.

Bank Reconciliation

2.

JOURNAL PAGE

	DATE		DESCRIPTION	POST. REF.	DEBIT	CREDIT	
1							1
2							2
3							3
4							4
5							5
6							6
7							7

PROBLEM 8-4 ___

1.

Bank Reconciliation

PROBLEM 8-4 ___, Concluded

2.

JOURNAL

PAGE

	DATE		DESCRIPTION	POST. REF.	DEBIT	CREDIT	
1							1
2							2
3							3
4							4
5							5
6							6
7							7
8							8
9							9
10							10
11							11
12							12
13							13
14							14
15							15
16							16
17							17
18							18
19							19
20							20
21							21
22							22
23							23
24							24
25							25
26							26
27							27
28							28
29							29
30							30
31							31
32							32
33							33
34							34
35							35
36							36

Name ______________________________

PROBLEM 8-5 ___

1.

Bank Reconciliation

PROBLEM 8-5 ___, Concluded

2.

JOURNAL

PAGE

	DATE		DESCRIPTION	POST. REF.	DEBIT	CREDIT	
1							1
2							2
3							3
4							4
5							5
6							6
7							7
8							8
9							9
10							10
11							11
12							12
13							13
14							14
15							15
16							16
17							17
18							18
19							19
20							20
21							21
22							22
23							23
24							24

3. ______________________

4.

Name

EXERCISE 9-1

EXERCISE 9-2

a.

b.

c.

EXERCISE 9-3

JOURNAL

PAGE

	DATE		DESCRIPTION	POST. REF.	DEBIT	CREDIT	
1							1
2							2
3							3
4							4
5							5
6							6
7							7
8							8
9							9
10							10
11							11
12							12
13							13
14							14
15							15
16							16
17							17
18							18
19							19
20							20

Name ______________________________

EXERCISE 9-4

JOURNAL PAGE

	DATE		DESCRIPTION	POST. REF.	DEBIT	CREDIT	
1							1
2							2
3							3
4							4
5							5
6							6
7							7
8							8
9							9
10							10
11							11
12							12
13							13
14							14
15							15
16							16
17							17

EXERCISE 9-5

a.–b.

JOURNAL PAGE

	DATE		DESCRIPTION	POST. REF.	DEBIT	CREDIT	
1							1
2							2
3							3
4							4
5							5
6							6
7							7
8							8
9							9
10							10

EXERCISE 9-6

a. ______________________

b. ______________________

c. ______________________

b. ______________________

EXERCISE 9-7

Account	Due Date	Number of Days Past Due
AAA Pickup Shop	May 30	
Best Auto	July 14	
Downtown Repair	March 18	
Luke's Auto Repair	June 1	
New or Used Auto	June 18	
Sally's	April 12	
Trident Auto	May 31	
Washburn Repair & Tow	March 13	

EXERCISE 9-8

a.

Customer	Due Date	Number of Days Past Due
Cottonwood Industries	July 6	
Fargo Company	September 17	
Garfield Inc.	October 17	
Sadler Company	November 2	
Twitty Company	December 23	

Name ______________________

EXERCISE 9-8, Concluded

	A	B	C	D	E	F	G
1	Aging of Receivables Schedule						
2	November 30						
3				Days Past Due			
4	Customer	Balance	Not Past Due	1–30	31–60	61–90	Over 90
5	Abbott Brothers Inc.	2,000	2,000				
6	Alonso Company	1,500		1,500			
21	Ziel Company	5,000			5,000		
22	Subtotals	807,500	475,000	180,000	78,500	42,300	31,700
23							
24							
25							
26							
27							
28							

EXERCISE 9-9

	BALANCE	NOT PAST DUE	DAYS PAST DUE			
			1–30	31–60	61–90	OVER 90

EXERCISE 9-10

JOURNAL PAGE

	DATE		DESCRIPTION	POST. REF.	DEBIT	CREDIT	
1							1
2							2
3							3
4							4
5							5

EXERCISE 9-11

Age Interval	Balance	Estimated Uncollectible Accounts Percent	Estimated Uncollectible Accounts Amount
Not past due	$567,000	½%	$
1–30 days past due	58,000	3	
31–60 days past due	29,000	7	
61–90 days past due	20,500	15	
91–180 days past due	15,000	40	
Over 180 days past due	10,500	75	
Total	$700,000		$

EXERCISE 9-12

JOURNAL PAGE

	DATE		DESCRIPTION	POST. REF.	DEBIT	CREDIT	
1							1
2							2
3							3
4							4
5							5

Name ________________________________

EXERCISE 9-13

a.

JOURNAL

PAGE ______

DATE		DESCRIPTION	POST. REF.	DEBIT	CREDIT

EXERCISE 9-13, Concluded

b.

JOURNAL

PAGE

DATE		DESCRIPTION	POST. REF.	DEBIT	CREDIT

c.

Name ____________________________________

EXERCISE 9-14

a.

JOURNAL

PAGE

	DATE		DESCRIPTION	POST. REF.	DEBIT	CREDIT	
1							1
2							2
3							3
4							4
5							5
6							6
7							7
8							8
9							9
10							10
11							11
12							12
13							13
14							14
15							15
16							16
17							17
18							18
19							19
20							20
21							21
22							22
23							23
24							24
25							25
26							26
27							27
28							28
29							29
30							30
31							31
32							32
33							33
34							34
35							35
36							36

EXERCISE 9-14, Continued

b.

JOURNAL

PAGE

	DATE		DESCRIPTION	POST. REF.	DEBIT	CREDIT	
1							1
2							2
3							3
4							4
5							5
6							6
7							7
8							8
9							9
10							10
11							11
12							12
13							13
14							14
15							15
16							16
17							17
18							18
19							19
20							20
21							21
22							22
23							23
24							24

EXERCISE 9-14, Concluded

Computations:

Aging Class (Number of Days Past Due)	Receivables Balance on Dec. 31	Estimated Doubtful Accounts: Percent	Estimated Doubtful Accounts: Amount
0–30 days	$200,000	2%	$
31–60 days	75,000	8	
61–90 days	24,000	25	
91–120 days	9,000	40	
More than 120 days	12,000	80	
Total receivables	$320,000		
			$

c.

EXERCISE 9-15

EXERCISE 9-16

a. ______________________________

b. ______________________________

EXERCISE 9-17

a.

JOURNAL PAGE

	DATE		DESCRIPTION	POST. REF.	DEBIT	CREDIT	
1							1
2							2
3							3
4							4
5							5
6							6

b.

JOURNAL PAGE

	DATE		DESCRIPTION	POST. REF.	DEBIT	CREDIT	
1							1
2							2
3							3
4							4
5							5
6							6
7							7
8							8
9							9
10							10

c. ____

____

____

____

Name ______________________________

EXERCISE 9-18

a.

JOURNAL PAGE

	DATE		DESCRIPTION	POST. REF.	DEBIT	CREDIT	
1							1
2							2
3							3
4							4
5							5
6							6

b.

JOURNAL PAGE

	DATE		DESCRIPTION	POST. REF.	DEBIT	CREDIT	
1							1
2							2
3							3
4							4
5							5
6							6
7							7
8							8
9							9
10							10

Computations:

		Estimated Doubtful Accounts	
Aging Class (Number of Days Past Due)	**Receivables Balance on Dec. 31**	**Percent**	**Amount**
0–30 days	$480,000	1%	$
31–60 days	100,000	3	
61–90 days	40,000	20	
91–120 days	25,000	30	
More than 120 days	5,000	40	
Total receivables	$650,000		
			$

EXERCISE 9-19

	Date of Note	Face Amount	Interest Rate	Term of Note	Due Date	Interest Due
a.	October 1	$ 10,500	8%	60 days	________	$ ________
b.	August 30	18,000	10	120 days	________	________
c.	May 30	12,000	12	90 days	________	________
d.	March 6	15,000	9	60 days	________	________
e.	May 23	9,000	10	60 days	________	________

EXERCISE 9-20

a. ______________________________

b. ______________________________

c. (1) and (2)

JOURNAL PAGE

	DATE		DESCRIPTION	POST. REF.	DEBIT	CREDIT	
1							1
2							2
3							3
4							4
5							5
6							6

EXERCISE 9-21

1. ______________________________
2. ______________________________
3. ______________________________
4. ______________________________
5. ______________________________
6. ______________________________

   ____
7. ______________________________

   ____

EXERCISE 9-22

JOURNAL

PAGE

	DATE		DESCRIPTION	POST. REF.	DEBIT	CREDIT	
1							1
2							2
3							3
4							4
5							5
6							6
7							7
8							8
9							9
10							10
11							11
12							12
13							13
14							14
15							15
16							16
17							17
18							18

EXERCISE 9-23

JOURNAL

PAGE

	DATE		DESCRIPTION	POST. REF.	DEBIT	CREDIT	
1							1
2							2
3							3
4							4
5							5
6							6
7							7
8							8
9							9
10							10
11							11

EXERCISE 9-24

JOURNAL

PAGE

	DATE		DESCRIPTION	POST. REF.	DEBIT	CREDIT	
1							1
2							2
3							3
4							4
5							5
6							6
7							7
8							8
9							9
10							10
11							11
12							12
13							13
14							14
15							15
16							16
17							17
18							18
19							19
20							20
21							21
22							22
23							23

EXERCISE 9-25

Optional

Balance Sheet

APPENDIX EXERCISE 9-26

a. ____________

b. ____________

c. ____________

d. ____________

e.

JOURNAL PAGE

	DATE		DESCRIPTION	POST. REF.	DEBIT	CREDIT	
1							1
2							2
3							3
4							4

APPENDIX EXERCISE 9-27

JOURNAL PAGE

	DATE		DESCRIPTION	POST. REF.	DEBIT	CREDIT	
1							1
2							2
3							3
4							4
5							5
6							6
7							7
8							8
9							9
10							10
11							11
12							12
13							13
14							14
15							15
16							16
17							17
18							18
19							19
20							20
21							21

EXERCISE 9-28

a. and b.

	2007	**2006**
Net sales	________	________
Accounts receivable	________	________
Average accounts receivable	________	________
Accounts receivable turnover	________	________
Average daily sales	________	________
Days' sales in receivables	________	________

c. ____________________

____

____

____

____

EXERCISE 9-29

a. 2007: ____________________

2006: ____________________

b. 2007: ____________________

2006: ____________________

c. ____________________

____

____

____

EXERCISE 9-30

a. and b.

	For the Period Ending	
	Feb. 3, 2007	**Jan. 28, 2006**
Net sales	________	________
Accounts receivable	________	________
Average accounts receivable	________	________
Accounts receivable turnover	________	________
Average daily sales	________	________
Days' sales in receivables	________	________

EXERCISE 9-30, Concluded

c. ______________________

EXERCISE 9-31

a. The Limited, Inc.:

H.J. Heinz Company:

b. ______________________

c. ______________________

PROBLEM 9-1 ___

1. and 2.

Allowance for Doubtful Accounts

Bad Debt Expense

3. ____________________

4. a. ____________________

   b. ____________________

   c. ____________________

PROBLEM 9-1 ___, Concluded

2.

JOURNAL

PAGE

DATE		DESCRIPTION	POST. REF.	DEBIT	CREDIT

Name ______________________

PROBLEM 9-2 ___

1.

Customer	Due Date	Number of Days Past Due

4.

JOURNAL PAGE

	DATE		DESCRIPTION	POST. REF.	DEBIT	CREDIT	
1							1
2							2
3							3
4							4
5							5
6							6
7							7

PROBLEM 9-2 ___, Concluded

2. and 3.

	A	B	C	D	E	F	G	H
1	Aging of Receivables Schedule							
2	December 31, 2009							
3				Days Past Due				
4	Customer	Balance	Not Past Due	1–30	31–60	61–90	Over 90	Over 120
5								
6								
30								
31								
32								
33								
34								
35								
36								
37								
38								
39								
40								
41								
42								

Name ______________________________

PROBLEM 9-3 ___

1.

Year	Bad Debt Expense			Balance of Allowance Account, End of Year
	Expense Actually Reported	Expense Based on Estimate	Increase (Decrease) in Amount of Expense	

2.

____

____

____

____

____

____

____

____

____

____

____

____

____

____

Name ______________________________

PROBLEM 9-4 ___

1.

Note	(a) Due Date	(b) Interest Due at Maturity
1.		
2.		
3.		
4.		
5.		
6.		

2., 3., and 4.

JOURNAL PAGE

	DATE		DESCRIPTION	POST. REF.	DEBIT	CREDIT	
1							1
2							2
3							3
4							4
5							5
6							6
7							7
8							8
9							9
10							10
11							11
12							12
13							13
14							14
15							15
16							16
17							17
18							18
19							19
20							20
21							21
22							22
23							23
24							24

Name ______________________________

PROBLEM 9-5 ___

JOURNAL

PAGE

	DATE		DESCRIPTION	POST. REF.	DEBIT	CREDIT	
1							1
2							2
3							3
4							4
5							5
6							6
7							7
8							8
9							9
10							10
11							11
12							12
13							13
14							14
15							15
16							16
17							17
18							18
19							19
20							20
21							21
22							22
23							23
24							24
25							25
26							26
27							27
28							28
29							29
30							30
31							31
32							32
33							33
34							34
35							35
36							36

Name ______________________

PROBLEM 9-6 ___

JOURNAL

PAGE

	DATE		DESCRIPTION	POST. REF.	DEBIT	CREDIT	
1							1
2							2
3							3
4							4
5							5
6							6
7							7
8							8
9							9
10							10
11							11
12							12
13							13
14							14
15							15
16							16
17							17
18							18
19							19
20							20
21							21
22							22
23							23
24							24
25							25
26							26
27							27
28							28
29							29
30							30
31							31
32							32
33							33
34							34
35							35
36							36

PROBLEM 9-6 ___, Concluded

JOURNAL

PAGE

DATE		DESCRIPTION	POST. REF.	DEBIT	CREDIT

Name ______________________________

EXERCISE 10-1

a. New printing press costs debited to the asset account:

b. Used printing press costs debited to the asset account:

EXERCISE 10-2

a.

b.

EXERCISE 10-3

EXERCISE 10-4

1. ______________________
2. ______________________
3. ______________________
4. ______________________
5. ______________________
6. ______________________
7. ______________________
8. ______________________
9. ______________________
10. ______________________

EXERCISE 10-5

1. ______________________
2. ______________________
3. ______________________
4. ______________________
5. ______________________
6. ______________________
7. ______________________
8. ______________________
9. ______________________
10. ______________________

EXERCISE 10-6

JOURNAL PAGE

	DATE		DESCRIPTION	POST. REF.	DEBIT	CREDIT	
1							1
2							2
3							3
4							4
5							5
6							6
7							7
8							8

Name ______________________

EXERCISE 10-7

a. ______________________

____

____

____

b. ______________________

____

____

____

EXERCISE 10-8

a. 2 years: ______________________

b. 8 years: ______________________

c. 10 years: ______________________

d. 20 years: ______________________

e. 25 years: ______________________

f. 40 years: ______________________

g. 50 years: ______________________

EXERCISE 10-9

____

____

EXERCISE 10-10

____

____

____

____

EXERCISE 10-11

a.

Truck No.	Rate per Mile	Miles Operated	Credit to Accumulated Depreciation
1	________	________	$________
2	________	________	$________
3	________	________	$________
4	________	________	$________
Total			$________

b.

JOURNAL PAGE

	DATE		DESCRIPTION	POST. REF.	DEBIT	CREDIT	
1							1
2							2
3							3

EXERCISE 10-12

a. Straight-line method:

First year: ______________________________

Second year: ______________________________

b. Double-declining-balance method:

First year: ______________________________

Second year: ______________________________

EXERCISE 10-13

a. Straight-line method:

____

b. Double-declining-balance method:

Year 1: ______________________________

Year 2: ______________________________

Name ______________________________

EXERCISE 10-14

a. Straight-line method:

Year 1: ______________________________

Year 2: ______________________________

b. Double-declining-balance method:

Year 1: ______________________________

Year 2: ______________________________

EXERCISE 10-15

a. ______________________________

b. ______________________________

c. ______________________________

EXERCISE 10-16

a. and b.

JOURNAL PAGE ______

	DATE		DESCRIPTION	POST. REF.	DEBIT	CREDIT	
1							1
2							2
3							3
4							4
5							5
6							6
7							7
8							8
9							9
10							10
11							11
12							12
13							13
14							14
15							15
16							16
17							17

EXERCISE 10-17

a.

b.(1) and (2)

JOURNAL

PAGE

	DATE		DESCRIPTION	POST. REF.	DEBIT	CREDIT	
1							1
2							2
3							3
4							4
5							5
6							6
7							7
8							8
9							9
17							17

EXERCISE 10-18

a. 2007: ____________________

2008: ____________________

2009: ____________________

b. ____________________

Name ______________________________

EXERCISE 10-18, Concluded

c. and d.

JOURNAL PAGE

	DATE		DESCRIPTION	POST. REF.	DEBIT	CREDIT	
1							1
2							2
3							3
4							4
5							5
6							6
7							7
8							8
9							9
10							10
11							11
12							12
13							13
14							14
15							15
16							16
17							17

EXERCISE 10-19

a. ______________________________

____

b.

JOURNAL PAGE

	DATE		DESCRIPTION	POST. REF.	DEBIT	CREDIT	
1							1
2							2
3							3
4							4

EXERCISE 10-20

a. ______________________________

b.

JOURNAL PAGE

	DATE		DESCRIPTION	POST. REF.	DEBIT	CREDIT	
1							1
2							2
3							3
4							4

EXERCISE 10-21

a.

	Current Year	*Preceding Year*

Name ______________________________

EXERCISE 10-21, Concluded

b.

EXERCISE 10-22

APPENDIX 1 EXERCISE 10-23

First year: ____

____

Second year.: ____

____

APPENDIX 1 EXERCISE 10-24

First year: ____

____

Second year: ____

____

APPENDIX 1 EXERCISE 10-25

First year: ____

____

Second year: ____

____

APPENDIX 2 EXERCISE 10-26

a.

b.

APPENDIX 2 EXERCISE 10-27

a.

APPENDIX 2 EXERCISE 10-27, Concluded

b.

APPENDIX 2 EXERCISE 10-28

a. and b.

JOURNAL

PAGE

	DATE		DESCRIPTION	POST. REF.	DEBIT	CREDIT	
1							1
2							2
3							3
4							4
5							5
6							6
7							7
8							8
9							9
10							10

APPENDIX 2 EXERCISE 10-29

a. and b.

JOURNAL

PAGE

	DATE		DESCRIPTION	POST. REF.	DEBIT	CREDIT	
1							1
2							2
3							3
4							4
5							5
6							6
7							7
8							8
9							9
10							10

EXERCISE 10-30

a. and b.

EXERCISE 10-31

a.

Best Buy:

Circuit City Stores, Inc:

b.

Name ______________________________

PROBLEM 10-1 ___

1. and 2.

Item	Land	Land Improvements	Building	Other Accounts
a.				
b.				
c.				
d.				
e.				
f.				
g.				
h.				
i.				
j.				
k.				
l.				
m.				
n.				
o.				
p.				
q.				
r.				
s.				
Total				

*Indicates receipt

3.

____

____

____

Name ______________________________

PROBLEM 10-2 ___

	Depreciation Expense		
Year	**a. Straight-Line Method**	**b. Units-of-Production Method**	**c. Double-Declining-Balance Method**
______	______	______	______
______	______	______	______
______	______	______	______
______	______	______	______
Total	______	______	______

Calculations:

Name ____________________

PROBLEM 10-3 ___

a.

Straight-Line Method

Year	Calculations	Depreciation Expense
2008		
2009		
2010		
2011		

b.

Units-of-Production Method

Year	Calculations	Depreciation Expense
2008		
2009		
2010		
2011		

c.

Double-Declining-Balance Method

Year	Calculations	Depreciation Expense
2008		
2009		
2010		
2011		

Name ____________________

PROBLEM 10-4 ___

1. a.

Straight-Line Method

Year	Depreciation Expense	Accumulated Depreciation, End of Year	Book Value, End of Year
1			
2			
3			
4			
5			

b.

Double-Declining-Balance Method

Year	Depreciation Expense	Accumulated Depreciation, End of Year	Book Value, End of Year
1			
2			
3			
4			
5			

PROBLEM 10-4 ___, Concluded

2.

JOURNAL

PAGE

	DATE		DESCRIPTION	POST. REF.	DEBIT	CREDIT	
1							1
2							2
3							3
4							4
5							5
6							6
7							7
8							8
9							9
10							10
11							11
12							12
13							13
14							14

3.

JOURNAL

PAGE

	DATE		DESCRIPTION	POST. REF.	DEBIT	CREDIT	
1							1
2							2
3							3
4							4
5							5
6							6
7							7
8							8
9							9
10							10
11							11
12							12
13							13
14							14

PROBLEM 10-5 ___

JOURNAL

PAGE

DATE		DESCRIPTION	POST. REF.	DEBIT	CREDIT

PROBLEM 10-5 ___, Concluded

JOURNAL

PAGE

DATE		DESCRIPTION	POST. REF.	DEBIT	CREDIT

PROBLEM 10-6 ___

1.

a. ______________________________

____

____

b. ______________________________

____

____

c. ______________________________

____

____

2.

JOURNAL PAGE

	DATE		DESCRIPTION	POST. REF.	DEBIT	CREDIT	
1							1
2							2
3							3
4							4
5							5
6							6
7							7
8							8
9							9
10							10
11							11
12							12

Name ______________________________

EXERCISE 11-1

EXERCISE 11-2

a.(1) through b.(2)

JOURNAL

PAGE

	DATE		DESCRIPTION	POST. REF.	DEBIT	CREDIT	
1							1
2							2
3							3
4							4
5							5
6							6
7							7
8							8
9							9
10							10
11							11
12							12
13							13
14							14
15							15
16							16
17							17
18							18
19							19
20							20

EXERCISE 11-3

a. ______________________________

____

b. (1) ______________________________

(2) ______________________________

c. ______________________________

EXERCISE 11-4

a. and b.

JOURNAL PAGE

	DATE		DESCRIPTION	POST. REF.	DEBIT	CREDIT	
1							1
2							2
3							3
4							4
5							5
6							6
7							7
8							8
9							9
10							10
11							11
12							12
13							13
14							14

Name ______________________________

EXERCISE 11-5

a. and b.

JOURNAL PAGE

	DATE		DESCRIPTION	POST. REF.	DEBIT	CREDIT	
1							1
2							2
3							3
4							4
5							5
6							6
7							7
8							8
9							9

EXERCISE 11-6

a.–c.

JOURNAL PAGE

	DATE		DESCRIPTION	POST. REF.	DEBIT	CREDIT	
1							1
2							2
3							3
4							4
5							5
6							6
7							7
8							8
9							9
10							10
11							11
12							12

EXERCISE 11-7

a. ______________________________

____

b. ______________________________

____

c. ______________________________

____

EXERCISE 11-8

a.

b.

EXERCISE 11-9

	Consultant	Computer Programmer	Administrator
Regular earnings	$	$	$
Overtime earnings			
Gross pay	$	$	$
Less: Social security tax	$	$	$
Medicare tax			
Federal income tax withheld			
	$	$	$
Net pay	$	$	$

EXERCISE 11-9, Concluded

Withholding Supporting Calculations

	Consultant	Computer Programmer	Administrator

EXERCISE 11-10

a.

EXERCISE 11-10, Concluded

b. and c.

JOURNAL PAGE

	DATE		DESCRIPTION	POST. REF.	DEBIT	CREDIT	
1							1
2							2
3							3
4							4
5							5
6							6
7							7
8							8
9							9
10							10
11							11
12							12

d. ____________________

EXERCISE 11-11

a.

EXERCISE 11-11, Concluded

b.

JOURNAL PAGE

	DATE		DESCRIPTION	POST. REF.	DEBIT	CREDIT	
1							1
2							2
3							3
4							4
5							5
6							6
7							7
8							8
9							9

EXERCISE 11-12

a.

JOURNAL PAGE

	DATE		DESCRIPTION	POST. REF.	DEBIT	CREDIT	
1							1
2							2
3							3
4							4
5							5
6							6
7							7
8							8

b.

JOURNAL PAGE

	DATE		DESCRIPTION	POST. REF.	DEBIT	CREDIT	
1							1
2							2
3							3
4							4
5							5
6							6
7							7
8							8

EXERCISE 11-13

a.

JOURNAL PAGE

	DATE		DESCRIPTION	POST. REF.	DEBIT	CREDIT	
1							1
2							2
3							3
4							4
5							5
6							6
7							7
8							8
9							9

b.

JOURNAL PAGE

	DATE		DESCRIPTION	POST. REF.	DEBIT	CREDIT	
1							1
2							2
3							3
4							4
5							5
6							6
7							7
8							8
9							9

EXERCISE 11-14

Name ______________________________

EXERCISE 11-15

a. ______________________________

b. ______________________________

c. ______________________________

d. ______________________________

e. ______________________________

EXERCISE 11-16

EXERCISE 11-17

JOURNAL PAGE

	DATE		DESCRIPTION	POST. REF.	DEBIT	CREDIT	
1							1
2							2
3							3

EXERCISE 11-18

a. and b.

JOURNAL PAGE

	DATE		DESCRIPTION	POST. REF.	DEBIT	CREDIT	
1							1
2							2
3							3
4							4
5							5
6							6

EXERCISE 11-19

EXERCISE 11-20

a. and b.

JOURNAL

PAGE

	DATE		DESCRIPTION	POST. REF.	DEBIT	CREDIT	
1							1
2							2
3							3
4							4
5							5
6							6
7							7
8							8

EXERCISE 11-21

a. ______________________

b.

JOURNAL PAGE

	DATE		DESCRIPTION	POST. REF.	DEBIT	CREDIT	
1							1
2							2
3							3
4							4
5							5

EXERCISE 11-22

a.

JOURNAL PAGE

	DATE		DESCRIPTION	POST. REF.	DEBIT	CREDIT	
1							1
2							2
3							3
4							4

b. ______________________

EXERCISE 11-23

a. December 31, 2009: ____________________

December 31, 2010: ____________________

b. ____________________

EXERCISE 11-24

a.

	Apple Computer, Inc:	Dell Inc.:
Quick Ratio:	________	________

Computations:

b.

Name ______________________________

PROBLEM 11-1 ___

1.

JOURNAL

PAGE

	DATE		DESCRIPTION	POST. REF.	DEBIT	CREDIT	
1							1
2							2
3							3
4							4
5							5
6							6
7							7
8							8
9							9
10							10
11							11
12							12
13							13
14							14
15							15
16							16
17							17
18							18
19							19
20							20
21							21
22							22
23							23
24							24
25							25
26							26
27							27
28							28
29							29
30							30
31							31
32							32
33							33
34							34
35							35
36							36

PROBLEM 11-1 ___, Concluded

1. and 2.

JOURNAL

PAGE

	DATE		DESCRIPTION	POST. REF.	DEBIT	CREDIT	
1							1
2							2
3							3
4							4
5							5
6							6
7							7
8							8
9							9
10							10
11							11
12							12
13							13
14							14
15							15
16							16
17							17
18							18
19							19
20							20
21							21
22							22
23							23
24							24
25							25
26							26
27							27
28							28
29							29
30							30
31							31
32							32
33							33
34							34
35							35
36							36

PROBLEM 11-2 ___

1.

JOURNAL

PAGE

	DATE		DESCRIPTION	POST. REF.	DEBIT	CREDIT	
1							1
2							2
3							3
4							4
5							5
6							6
7							7
8							8
9							9
10							10
11							11
12							12
13							13
14							14
15							15
16							16
17							17
18							18
19							19
20							20
21							21
22							22
23							23
24							24
25							25
26							26
27							27
28							28
29							29
30							30
31							31
32							32
33							33
34							34
35							35
36							36

PROBLEM 11-2 ___, Concluded

2.

JOURNAL

PAGE

	DATE		DESCRIPTION	POST. REF.	DEBIT	CREDIT	
1							1
2							2
3							3
4							4
5							5
6							6
7							7
8							8
9							9
10							10
11							11
12							12
13							13
14							14
15							15
16							16
17							17
18							18
19							19
20							20
21							21
22							22
23							23
24							24
25							25
26							26
27							27
28							28
29							29
30							30
31							31
32							32
33							33
34							34
35							35
36							36

Name ________________________________

PROBLEM 11-3 ___

1.

Employee	Gross Earnings	Federal Income Tax Withheld	Social Security Tax Withheld	Medicare Tax Withheld

____

____

____

____

____

PROBLEM 11-3 ___, Concluded

2. Payroll taxes incurred and paid by employer:

a. Social security tax paid by employer .... $ ______________

b. Medicare tax paid by employer .... ______________

c. State unemployment compensation tax .... ______________

Calculations and comments:

____

____

____

____

____

____

d. Federal unemployment compensation tax .... ______________

e. Total payroll tax expense .... $ ______________

PROBLEM 11-4A

PAYROLL FOR THE WEEK ENDED *September 12, 2010*

Name	Total Hours	EARNINGS			DEDUCTION					PAID		ACCOUNTS DEBITED		
		Regular	Over-time	Total	Social Security Tax	Medicare Tax	Federal Income Tax	Medical Insurance	Total	Net Pay	Ck. No.	Sales Salaries Expense	Office Salaries Expense	Delivery Salaries Expense
Baron, Red	42	800.00	60.00	860.00	51.60	12.90	137.60	65.00	267.10	592.90	801	860.00		
Brown, Charles	46	880.00	198.00	1,078.00	64.68	16.17	161.70	74.00	316.55	761.45	802	1,078.00		
Davis, Marci	40	840.00		840.00	50.40	12.60	121.80	59.00	243.80	596.20	803			840.00
Johnson, Franklin		2,400.00		2,400.00	0.00	36.00	456.00	125.00	617.00	1,783.00	804		2,400.00	
Lewis, Lucy	45	1,040.00	195.00	1,235.00	74.10	18.53	216.13	96.00	404.76	830.24	805	1,235.00		
Mint, Patricia		1,850.00		1,850.00	111.00	27.75	333.00	115.00	586.75	1,263.25	806	1,850.00		
Shultz, Chuck	48	1,000.00	300.00	1,300.00	78.00	19.50	227.50	98.00	423.00	877.00	807		1,300.00	
Shroeder, Ivan	50	920.00	345.00	1,265.00	75.90	18.98	215.05	87.00	396.93	868.07	808			1,265.00
Van Pelt, Linus	38	608.00		608.00	36.48	9.12	76.00	78.00	199.60	408.40	809			608.00
		10,338.00	1,098.00	11,436.00	542.16	171.55	1,944.78	797.00	3,455.49	7,980.51		5,023.00	3,700.00	2,713.00

PROBLEM 11-4B

PAYROLL FOR THE WEEK ENDED *September 12, 2010*

		EARNINGS			DEDUCTION					PAID		ACCOUNTS DEBITED		
Name	Total Hours	Regular	Over-time	Total	Social Secu-rity Tax	Medi-care Tax	Federal Income Tax	Medi-cal Insur-ance	Total	Net Pay	Ck. No.	Sales Salaries Expense	Office Salaries Expense	Delivery Salaries Expense
Baron, Red	44	1,000.00	150.00	1,150.00	69.00	17.25	184.00	74.00	344.25	805.75	401	1,150.00		
Brown, Charles	43	1,120.00	126.00	1,246.00	74.76	18.69	186.90	82.00	362.35	883.65	402	1,246.00		
Davis, Marci	40	960.00		960.00	57.60	14.40	139.20	68.00	270.20	680.80	403			960.00
Johnson, Franklin		3,000.00		3,000.00	0.00	45.00	570.00	130.00	745.00	2,255.00	404		3,000.00	
Lewis, Lucy	47	1,120.00	294.00	1,414.00	84.84	21.21	247.45	110.00	463.50	950.50	405	1,414.00		
Mint, Patricia		2,200.00		2,200.00	0.00	33.00	396.00	121.00	550.00	1,650.00	406	2,200.00		
Shultz, Chuck	46	1,200.00	270.00	1,470.00	88.20	22.05	257.25	96.00	463.50	1,006.50	407		1,470.00	
Shroeder, Ivan	52	1,120.00	504.00	1,624.00	97.44	24.36	276.08	92.00	489.88	1,134.12	408			1,624.00
Van Pelt, Linus	36	648.00		648.00	38.88	9.72	81.00	81.00	210.60	437.40	409			648.00
		12,368.00	1,344.00	13,712.00	510.72	205.68	2,337.88	854.00	3,908.28	9,803.72		6,010.00	4,470.00	3,232.00

PROBLEM 11-4 ___, Concluded

1.–4.

JOURNAL

PAGE

	DATE		DESCRIPTION	POST. REF.	DEBIT	CREDIT	
1							1
2							2
3							3
4							4
5							5
6							6
7							7
8							8
9							9
10							10
11							11
12							12
13							13
14							14
15							15
16							16
17							17
18							18
19							19
20							20
21							21
22							22
23							23
24							24
25							25
26							26
27							27
28							28
29							29
30							30
31							31
32							32
33							33
34							34
35							35
36							36

PROBLEM 11-5 ___

1. *The payroll register form is on pages 472-473.*

2.

JOURNAL PAGE

	DATE		DESCRIPTION	POST. REF.	DEBIT	CREDIT	
1							1
2							2
3							3
4							4
5							5
6							6
7							7
8							8
9							9
10							10

PROBLEM 11-5 ___, Continued

1.

PAYROLL FOR WEEK ENDING

	NAME	TOTAL HOURS	EARNINGS			DEDUCTIONS		
			REGULAR	OVERTIME	TOTAL	SOCIAL SECURITY TAX	MEDICARE TAX	
1								1
2								2
3								3
4								4
5								5
6								6
7								7
8								8
9								9
10								10
11								11
12								12
13								13
14								14
15								15
16								16
17								17
18								18
19								19
20								20
21								21
22								22
23								23
24								24
25								25
26								26
27								27
28								28
29								29
30								30
31								31
32								32
33								33

PROBLEM 11-5 ___, Concluded

December 10, 2010

			PAID		ACCOUNTS DEBITED	
FEDERAL INCOME TAX	U.S. SAVINGS BONDS	TOTAL	NET PAY	CK. NO.	SALES SALARIES EXPENSE	OFFICE SALARIES EXPENSE

Name ____________________

PROBLEM 11-6 ___

1.

JOURNAL

PAGE

DATE		DESCRIPTION	POST. REF.	DEBIT	CREDIT

PROBLEM 11-6 ___, Continued

JOURNAL

PAGE

DATE		DESCRIPTION	POST. REF.	DEBIT	CREDIT

PROBLEM 11-6 ___, Concluded

2.

JOURNAL

PAGE

	DATE		DESCRIPTION	POST. REF.	DEBIT	CREDIT	
1							1
2							2
3							3
4							4
5							5
6							6
7							7
8							8
9							9
10							10
11							11
12							12
13							13
14							14
15							15
16							16
17							17
18							18
19							19
20							20
21							21
22							22
23							23
24							24
25							25
26							26
27							27
28							28
29							29
30							30
31							31
32							32
33							33
34							34
35							35
36							36

Name ______________________________

COMPREHENSIVE PROBLEM 3

1.

JOURNAL

PAGE

DATE		DESCRIPTION	POST. REF.	DEBIT	CREDIT

COMPREHENSIVE PROBLEM 3, Continued

JOURNAL

PAGE

DATE		DESCRIPTION	POST. REF.	DEBIT	CREDIT

COMPREHENSIVE PROBLEM 3, Continued

2.

Bank Reconciliation

COMPREHENSIVE PROBLEM 3, Continued

3. and 4.

JOURNAL

PAGE

	DATE		DESCRIPTION	POST. REF.	DEBIT	CREDIT	
1							1
2							2
3							3
4							4
5							5
6							6
7							7
8							8
9							9
10							10
11							11
12							12
13							13
14							14
15							15
16							16
17							17
18							18
19							19
20							20
21							21
22							22
23							23
24							24
25							25
26							26
27							27
28							28
29							29
30							30
31							31
32							32
33							33
34							34
35							35
36							36

COMPREHENSIVE PROBLEM 3, Continued

JOURNAL

PAGE

	DATE		DESCRIPTION	POST. REF.	DEBIT	CREDIT	
1							1
2							2
3							3
4							4
5							5
6							6
7							7
8							8
9							9
10							10
11							11
12							12
13							13
14							14
15							15
16							16
17							17
18							18
19							19
20							20
21							21
22							22
23							23
24							24
25							25
26							26
27							27
28							28
29							29
30							30
31							31
32							32
33							33
34							34
35							35
36							36

COMPREHENSIVE PROBLEM 3, Continued

5.

Balance Sheet

Name ______________________

COMPREHENSIVE PROBLEM 3, Continued

COMPREHENSIVE PROBLEM 3, Concluded

6.

Name ______________________________

EXERCISE 12-1

JOURNAL PAGE

	DATE		DESCRIPTION	POST. REF.	DEBIT	CREDIT	
1							1
2							2
3							3
4							4
5							5
6							6

EXERCISE 12-2

JOURNAL PAGE

	DATE		DESCRIPTION	POST. REF.	DEBIT	CREDIT	
1							1
2							2
3							3
4							4
5							5
6							6
7							7
8							8
9							9

EXERCISE 12-3

	Hassell	Lawson
a.	____________	____________
b.	____________	____________
c.	____________	____________
d.	____________	____________
e.	____________	____________

Details

	Hassell	Lawson	Total
a.			
b.			
c.			
d.			
e.			

Name ______________________________

EXERCISE 12-4

	Hassell	Lawson
a.	____________	____________
b.	____________	____________
c.	____________	____________
d.	____________	____________
e.	____________	____________

Details

	Hassell	Lawson	Total
a.			
b.			
c.			
d.			
e.			

EXERCISE 12-5

	Casey Fisher	Logan Baylor	Total

EXERCISE 12-6

EXERCISE 12-7

a.

	Bowman	Mapes	Total

EXERCISE 12-7, Concluded

b. (1) and (2)

JOURNAL PAGE

	DATE		DESCRIPTION	POST. REF.	DEBIT	CREDIT	
1							1
2							2
3							3
4							4
5							5
6							6
7							7
8							8
9							9
10							10
11							11

EXERCISE 12-8

a.

	WYXT Partners	Lindsey Wilson	Daily Sun Newspaper, LLC	Total

EXERCISE 12-8 Concluded

b.

JOURNAL

PAGE

	DATE		DESCRIPTION	POST. REF.	DEBIT	CREDIT	
1							1
2							2
3							3
4							4
5							5
6							6
7							7
8							8
9							9
10							10
11							11
12							12

c.

Statement of Members' Equity

	WYXT Partners	Lindsey Wilson	Daily Sun Newspaper, LLC	Total

Name ______________________________

EXERCISE 12-9

a.–c.

JOURNAL PAGE

	DATE		DESCRIPTION	POST. REF.	DEBIT	CREDIT	
1							1
2							2
3							3
4							4
5							5
6							6
7							7
8							8
9							9
10							10
11							11
12							12

EXERCISE 12-10

a. and b.

JOURNAL PAGE

	DATE		DESCRIPTION	POST. REF.	DEBIT	CREDIT	
1							1
2							2
3							3

____

____

____

EXERCISE 12-11

a. ______________________________

b. ______________________________

____

c. ______________________________

____

____

EXERCISE 12-12

a. (1) and (2)

JOURNAL PAGE

	DATE		DESCRIPTION	POST. REF.	DEBIT	CREDIT	
1							1
2							2
3							3
4							4
5							5
6							6
7							7
8							8

b. ______________________

EXERCISE 12-13

a.

JOURNAL PAGE

	DATE		DESCRIPTION	POST. REF.	DEBIT	CREDIT	
1							1
2							2
3							3
4							4
5							5
6							6
7							7
8							8

b. ______________________

Name ______________________

EXERCISE 12-14

a.

JOURNAL PAGE

	DATE		DESCRIPTION	POST. REF.	DEBIT	CREDIT	
1							1
2							2
3							3
4							4
5							5
6							6

b. (1)

JOURNAL PAGE

	DATE		DESCRIPTION	POST. REF.	DEBIT	CREDIT	
1							1
2							2
3							3
4							4
5							5
6							6

Supporting calculations for the bonus:

EXERCISE 12-14, Concluded

b. (2)

JOURNAL PAGE

	DATE		DESCRIPTION	POST. REF.	DEBIT	CREDIT	
1							1
2							2
3							3
4							4
5							5
6							6

Supporting calculations for the bonus:

EXERCISE 12-15

a.

JOURNAL PAGE

	DATE		DESCRIPTION	POST. REF.	DEBIT	CREDIT	
1							1
2							2
3							3
4							4

Name ______________________________

EXERCISE 12-15, Continued

b. (1)

JOURNAL

PAGE

	DATE		DESCRIPTION	POST. REF.	DEBIT	CREDIT	
1							1
2							2
3							3
4							4

Supporting calculations for the bonus:

b. (2)

JOURNAL

PAGE

	DATE		DESCRIPTION	POST. REF.	DEBIT	CREDIT	
1							1
2							2
3							3
4							4

Supporting calculations for the bonus:

EXERCISE 12-16

Statement of Partnership Equity

	Jen Wilson, Capital	Teresa McDonald, Capital	Jaime Holden, Capital	Total Partnership Capital

Calculations

Admission of Jaime Holden:

Net income distribution:

Withdrawals:

Name ____________________

EXERCISE 12-17

a. and b.

JOURNAL PAGE

	DATE		DESCRIPTION	POST. REF.	DEBIT	CREDIT	
1							1
2							2
3							3
4							4
5							5
6							6
7							7
8							8
9							9
10							10
11							11
12							12

EXERCISE 12-18

a.–e.

EXERCISE 12-18, Concluded

EXERCISE 12-19

a.

b. and c.

	Pryor	Lester

EXERCISE 12-20

	Bradley	Barak	Total

EXERCISE 12-21

a. ______________________________

b. ______________________________

c.

JOURNAL PAGE

	DATE		DESCRIPTION	POST. REF.	DEBIT	CREDIT	
1							1
2							2
3							3

Supporting calculations:

	Matthews	Williams	Shen

EXERCISE 12-22

a.

	Houston	Alsup	Cross	Total

b.

	Houston	Alsup	Cross	Total

EXERCISE 12-23

	Hilliard	Downey	Petrov

EXERCISE 12-24

Statement of Partnership Liquidation

	CASH	NONCASH ASSETS	LIABILITIES	CAPITAL		
				DOVER	GOLL	CHAMBERLAND

Name ____________________ *Chapter 12*

EXERCISE 12-25

a.

Statement of LLC Liquidation

	CASH	NONCASH ASSETS	LIABILITIES	MEMBER EQUITY		
				GORDON	HIGHTOWER	MILLS

b.

JOURNAL PAGE

	DATE		DESCRIPTION	POST. REF.	DEBIT	CREDIT	
1							1
2							2
3							3
4							4
5							5

EXERCISE 12-26

a. (1) and (2)

JOURNAL PAGE

DATE		DESCRIPTION	POST. REF.	DEBIT	CREDIT

b.

Statement of Partners' Equity

	Hossam Abdel-Raja	Aly Meyer	Total

EXERCISE 12-27

a.

b.

EXERCISE 12-28

a.

b.

PROBLEM 12-1___

1.

JOURNAL

PAGE

DATE		DESCRIPTION	POST. REF.	DEBIT	CREDIT

2.

Balance Sheet

PROBLEM 12-1___, Concluded

3.

JOURNAL PAGE

	DATE		DESCRIPTION	POST. REF.	DEBIT	CREDIT	
1							1
2							2
3							3
4							4
5							5
6							6
7							7
8							8
9							9
10							10
11							11
12							12
13							13
14							14
15							15
16							16
17							17
18							18

Computations:

Name ____________________________________

PROBLEM 12-2___

	(1)		(2)	
Plan	Net Income of ________________		Net Income of ________________	
a.				
b.				
c.				
d.				
e.				
f.				

Supporting calculations:

	Net Income of ________________		Net Income of ________________	

PROBLEM 12-2___, Concluded

	Net Income of ____________		Net Income of ____________	

PROBLEM 12-3___

1.

Income Statement

Division of net income:

2.

Statement of Partners' Equity

PROBLEM 12-3___, Concluded

3.

Balance Sheet

Name ______________________________

PROBLEM 12-4 ___

1. and 2.

JOURNAL

PAGE

DATE		DESCRIPTION	POST. REF.	DEBIT	CREDIT

PROBLEM 12-4___, Concluded

3.

Balance Sheet

Name ____________________

PROBLEM 12-5___

1.

Statement of Partnership Liquidation

	CASH	NONCASH ASSETS	LIABILITIES	CAPITAL		

PROBLEM 12-5___, Concluded

2. a.

JOURNAL PAGE

	DATE		DESCRIPTION	POST. REF.	DEBIT	CREDIT	
1							1
2							2
3							3
4							4

2. b.

JOURNAL PAGE

	DATE		DESCRIPTION	POST. REF.	DEBIT	CREDIT	
1							1
2							2
3							3
4							4

Name ______________________________

PROBLEM 12-6___

1. a.

Statement of Partnership Liquidation

	CASH	NONCASH ASSETS	LIABILITIES	CAPITAL		

Name ______________________

PROBLEM 12-6___, Continued

1. b.

Statement of Partnership Liquidation

	CASH	NONCASH ASSETS	LIABILITIES	CAPITAL		

Name ________________________________

PROBLEM 12-6___, Concluded

2. a.

JOURNAL PAGE

	DATE		DESCRIPTION	POST. REF.	DEBIT	CREDIT	
1							1
2							2
3							3
4							4

2. b.

JOURNAL PAGE

	DATE		DESCRIPTION	POST. REF.	DEBIT	CREDIT	
1							1
2							2
3							3
4							4

Name ______________________________

EXERCISE 13-1

Description	1st Year	2nd Year	3rd Year	4th Year
Total dividend declared				
Preferred dividend (current)				
Preferred dividend in arrears				
Total preferred dividends				
Preferred shares outstanding				
Preferred dividend per share				
Dividend for common shares				
Common shares outstanding				
Common dividend per share				

EXERCISE 13-2

Description	1st Year	2nd Year	3rd Year	4th Year
Total dividend declared				
Preferred dividend (current)				
Preferred dividend in arrears				
Total preferred dividends				
Preferred shares outstanding				
Preferred dividend per share				
Dividend for common shares				
Common shares outstanding				
Common dividend per share				

EXERCISE 13-3

a.

JOURNAL PAGE

	DATE		DESCRIPTION	POST. REF.	DEBIT	CREDIT	
1							1
2							2
3							3
4							4
5							5
6							6
7							7
8							8
9							9
10							10

b. ____

EXERCISE 13-4

a.

JOURNAL PAGE

	DATE		DESCRIPTION	POST. REF.	DEBIT	CREDIT	
1							1
2							2
3							3
4							4
5							5
6							6
7							7
8							8
9							9
10							10

b. ____

EXERCISE 13-5

JOURNAL PAGE

	DATE		DESCRIPTION	POST. REF.	DEBIT	CREDIT	
1							1
2							2
3							3
4							4

EXERCISE 13-6

a.–c.

JOURNAL PAGE

	DATE		DESCRIPTION	POST. REF.	DEBIT	CREDIT	
1							1
2							2
3							3
4							4
5							5
6							6
7							7
8							8
9							9
10							10
11							11
12							12
13							13
14							14
15							15

EXERCISE 13-7

JOURNAL

PAGE

	DATE		DESCRIPTION	POST. REF.	DEBIT	CREDIT	
1							1
2							2
3							3
4							4
5							5
6							6
7							7
8							8
9							9

EXERCISE 13-8

JOURNAL

PAGE

	DATE		DESCRIPTION	POST. REF.	DEBIT	CREDIT	
1							1
2							2
3							3
4							4
5							5
6							6
7							7
8							8
9							9
10							10
11							11
12							12
13							13
14							14
15							15
16							16
17							17
18							18

Name ______________________________

EXERCISE 13-9

JOURNAL PAGE

	DATE		DESCRIPTION	POST. REF.	DEBIT	CREDIT	
1							1
2							2
3							3
4							4
5							5
6							6
7							7
8							8
9							9

EXERCISE 13-10

a. (1) and (2)

JOURNAL PAGE

	DATE		DESCRIPTION	POST. REF.	DEBIT	CREDIT	
1							1
2							2
3							3
4							4
5							5
6							6
7							7
8							8
9							9

b. **(1)** Total paid-in capital: ______________________________

(2) Total retained earnings: ______________________________

(3) Total stockholders' equity: ______________________________

c. **(1)** Total paid-in capital: ______________________________

(2) Total retained earnings: ______________________________

(3) Total stockholders' equity: ______________________________

EXERCISE 13-11

a.

JOURNAL PAGE

	DATE		DESCRIPTION	POST. REF.	DEBIT	CREDIT	
1							1
2							2
3							3
4							4
5							5
6							6
7							7
8							8
9							9
10							10
11							11
12							12
13							13

b. ______________________________

c. ______________________________

Name ______________________

EXERCISE 13-12

a.

JOURNAL

PAGE

	DATE		DESCRIPTION	POST. REF.	DEBIT	CREDIT	
1							1
2							2
3							3
4							4
5							5
6							6
7							7
8							8
9							9
10							10
11							11
12							12
13							13
14							14
15							15

b. ______________________

c. ______________________

d. ______________________

EXERCISE 13-13

a.

JOURNAL PAGE

	DATE		DESCRIPTION	POST. REF.	DEBIT	CREDIT	
1							1
2							2
3							3
4							4
5							5
6							6
7							7
8							8
9							9
10							10
11							11
12							12
13							13
14							14
15							15
16							16
17							17
18							18
19							19

b. ______________________

c. ______________________

d. ______________________

Name ______________________________

EXERCISE 13-14

EXERCISE 13-15

EXERCISE 13-16

EXERCISE 13-17

Retained Earnings Statement

Name ______________________________

EXERCISE 13-18

Corrected Stockholders' Equity section (optional):

EXERCISE 13-19

Statement of Stockholders' Equity

EXERCISE 13-20

a. ______________________

b. ______________________

EXERCISE 13-21

	Assets	Liabilities	Stockholders' Equity
(1) Declaring a cash dividend	______	______	______
(2) Paying the cash dividend declared in (1)	______	______	______
(3) Authorizing and issuing stock certificates in a stock split	______	______	______
(4) Declaring a stock dividend	______	______	______
(5) Issuing stock certificates for the stock dividend declared in (4)	______	______	______

EXERCISE 13-22

JOURNAL

PAGE

DATE		DESCRIPTION	POST. REF.	DEBIT	CREDIT

EXERCISE 13-23

EXERCISE 13-24

a.

b.

	2007	2006	2005

EXERCISE 13-25

a. Office Max: ______________________

Staples: ______________________

b. ______________________

PROBLEM 13-1 ___

1.

Year	Total Dividends	Preferred Dividends		Common Dividends	
		Total	Per Share	Total	Per Share
2005					
2006					
2007					
2008					
2009					
2010					

2.

Average annual dividend for preferred:

Average annual dividend for common:

3. a. ______________________

b. ______________________

Name ______________________________

PROBLEM 13-2 ___

JOURNAL

PAGE

	DATE		DESCRIPTION	POST. REF.	DEBIT	CREDIT	
1							1
2							2
3							3
4							4
5							5
6							6
7							7
8							8
9							9
10							10
11							11
12							12
13							13
14							14
15							15
16							16
17							17
18							18
19							19
20							20
21							21
22							22
23							23
24							24
25							25
26							26
27							27
28							28
29							29
30							30
31							31
32							32
33							33
34							34
35							35
36							36

Name ____________________________________

PROBLEM 13-3 ___

a.–g.

JOURNAL

PAGE

DATE		DESCRIPTION	POST. REF.	DEBIT	CREDIT

Name ______________________________

PROBLEM 13-4 ___

1. and 2.

Common Stock

Paid-In Capital in Excess of Stated Value

Retained Earnings

Treasury Stock

Paid-In Capital from Sale of Treasury Stock

PROBLEM 13-4 ___, Continued

Stock Dividends Distributable

Stock Dividends

Cash Dividends

Name ______________________________

PROBLEM 13-4 ___, Continued

2.

JOURNAL

PAGE

	DATE		DESCRIPTION	POST. REF.	DEBIT	CREDIT	
1							1
2							2
3							3
4							4
5							5
6							6
7							7
8							8
9							9
10							10
11							11
12							12
13							13
14							14
15							15
16							16
17							17
18							18
19							19
20							20
21							21
22							22
23							23
24							24
25							25
26							26
27							27
28							28
29							29
30							30
31							31
32							32
33							33
34							34
35							35
36							36

PROBLEM 13-4 ___, Concluded

3.

Retained Earnings Statement

4.

Name ______________________________

PROBLEM 13-5 ___

JOURNAL

PAGE

DATE		DESCRIPTION	POST. REF.	DEBIT	CREDIT

PROBLEM 13-5 ___, Concluded

JOURNAL

PAGE

	DATE		DESCRIPTION	POST. REF.	DEBIT	CREDIT	
1							1
2							2
3							3
4							4
5							5
6							6
7							7
8							8
9							9
10							10
11							11
12							12
13							13
14							14
15							15
16							16
17							17
18							18
19							19
20							20
21							21
22							22
23							23
24							24
25							25
26							26
27							27
28							28
29							29
30							30
31							31
32							32
33							33
34							34
35							35
36							36

EXERCISE 14-1

	a.	b.	c.
Earnings before bond interest and income tax			
Bond interest			
Balance			
Income tax			
Net income			
Dividends on preferred stock			
Earnings available for common stock			
Earnings per share on common stock			

EXERCISE 14-2

EXERCISE 14-3

EXERCISE 14-4

EXERCISE 14-5

JOURNAL PAGE

	DATE		DESCRIPTION	POST. REF.	DEBIT	CREDIT	
1							1
2							2
3							3
4							4
5							5
6							6
7							7
8							8
9							9
10							10

Name ____________________

EXERCISE 14-6

a. 1.–4.

JOURNAL PAGE

	DATE		DESCRIPTION	POST. REF.	DEBIT	CREDIT	
1							1
2							2
3							3
4							4
5							5
6							6
7							7
8							8
9							9
10							10
11							11
12							12
13							13

b.

EXERCISE 14-7

a. and b.

JOURNAL PAGE

	DATE		DESCRIPTION	POST. REF.	DEBIT	CREDIT	
1							1
2							2
3							3
4							4
5							5
6							6
7							7
8							8
9							9
10							10

EXERCISE 14-8

JOURNAL

PAGE

	DATE		DESCRIPTION	POST. REF.	DEBIT	CREDIT	
1							1
2							2
3							3
4							4
5							5
6							6
7							7
8							8
9							9
10							10
11							11
12							12
13							13

EXERCISE 14-9

JOURNAL

PAGE

	DATE		DESCRIPTION	POST. REF.	DEBIT	CREDIT	
1							1
2							2
3							3
4							4
5							5
6							6
7							7
8							8
9							9
10							10
11							11
12							12
13							13

EXERCISE 14-10

a. 1. and 2.

JOURNAL

PAGE

	DATE		DESCRIPTION	POST. REF.	DEBIT	CREDIT	
1							1
2							2
3							3
4							4
5							5
6							6
7							7
8							8
9							9
10							10

b. ______________________________

EXERCISE 14-11

JOURNAL

PAGE

	DATE		DESCRIPTION	POST. REF.	DEBIT	CREDIT	
1							1
2							2
3							3
4							4
5							5
6							6
7							7
8							8
9							9
10							10
11							11
12							12
13							13
14							14
15							15
16							16
17							17
18							18

EXERCISE 14-12

a.

Amortization of Installment Notes					
	A	B	C	D	E
For the Year Ending	January 1 Carrying Amount	Note Payment (Cash Paid)	Interest Expense (6.5% of January 1 Note Carrying Amount)	Decrease in Notes Payable (B – C)	December 31 Carrying Amount (A – D)

b.

JOURNAL

PAGE

DATE		DESCRIPTION	POST. REF.	DEBIT	CREDIT

EXERCISE 14-12, Concluded

JOURNAL

PAGE

	DATE		DESCRIPTION	POST. REF.	DEBIT	CREDIT	
1							1
2							2
3							3
4							4
5							5
6							6
7							7
8							8
9							9
10							10
11							11
12							12
13							13

EXERCISE 14-13

APPENDIX 1 EXERCISE 14-14

a. ____________________

b. ____________________

APPPENDIX 1 EXERCISE 14-15

a. ____________________

b. ____________________

APPENDIX 1 EXERCISE 14-16

____

APPENDIX 1 EXERCISE 14-17

____

Name ______________________________

APPENDIX 1 EXERCISE 14-18

APPENDIX 1 EXERCISE 14-19

APPENDIX 2 EXERCISE 14-20

a.

JOURNAL

PAGE

	DATE		DESCRIPTION	POST. REF.	DEBIT	CREDIT	
1							1
2							2
3							3
4							4
5							5
6							6
7							7
8							8
9							9
10							10
11							11
12							12
13							13

Computations:

b.

Name ______________________________

APPENDIX 2 EXERCISE 14-21

a.

JOURNAL PAGE

	DATE		DESCRIPTION	POST. REF.	DEBIT	CREDIT	
1							1
2							2
3							3
4							4
5							5
6							6
7							7
8							8
9							9
10							10
11							11
12							12
13							13
14							14
15							15

b.

APPENDIX 2 EXERCISE 14-22

a.–d.

Name ______________________________

APPENDIX 2 EXERCISE 14-23

a.–d.

EXERCISE 14-24

a. Current year: ______________________

____

Preceding year: ______________________

____

b. ______________________

____

____

____

____

PROBLEM 14-1 ___

1.

	Plan 1	Plan 2	Plan 3
Earnings before interest and income tax			
Deduct interest on bonds			
Income before income tax			
Deduct income tax			
Net income			
Dividends on preferred stock			
Available for dividends on common stock			
Shares of common stock outstanding			
Earnings per share on common stock			

2.

	Plan 1	Plan 2	Plan 3
Earnings before interest and income tax			
Deduct interest on bonds			
Income before income tax			
Deduct income tax			
Net income			
Dividends on preferred stock			
Available for dividends on common stock			
Shares of common stock outstanding			
Earnings per share on common stock			

PROBLEM 14-1 ___, Concluded

3.

Name ____________________

PROBLEM 14-2 ___

1. and 2.

JOURNAL

PAGE

	DATE		DESCRIPTION	POST. REF.	DEBIT	CREDIT	
1							1
2							2
3							3
4							4
5							5
6							6
7							7
8							8
9							9
10							10
11							11
12							12
13							13
14							14
15							15
16							16
17							17
18							18
19							19
20							20
21							21
22							22
23							23
24							24
25							25

3.

____

____

PROBLEM 14-2 ___, Concluded

4.

5.

PROBLEM 14-3 ___

1. and 2.

JOURNAL

PAGE

DATE		DESCRIPTION	POST. REF.	DEBIT	CREDIT

3.

____

____

PROBLEM 14-3 ___, Concluded

4.

____

____

____

____

____

5.

Name ____________________

PROBLEM 14-4 ___

1.

JOURNAL

PAGE

	DATE		DESCRIPTION	POST. REF.	DEBIT	CREDIT	
1							1
2							2
3							3
4							4
5							5
6							6
7							7
8							8
9							9
10							10
11							11
12							12
13							13
14							14
15							15
16							16
17							17
18							18
19							19
20							20
21							21
22							22
23							23
24							24
25							25
26							26
27							27
28							28
29							29
30							30
31							31
32							32
33							33
34							34
35							35
36							36

PROBLEM 14-4 ___, Concluded

JOURNAL

PAGE

	DATE		DESCRIPTION	POST. REF.	DEBIT	CREDIT	
1							1
2							2
3							3
4							4
5							5
6							6
7							7
8							8
9							9
10							10
11							11
12							12
13							13
14							14
15							15

2. (a) 2010: ______________________________

(b) 2011: ______________________________

3.

APPENDIX 2 PROBLEM 14-5 ___

1. and 2.

JOURNAL PAGE

	DATE		DESCRIPTION	POST. REF.	DEBIT	CREDIT	
1							1
2							2
3							3
4							4
5							5
6							6
7							7
8							8
9							9
10							10
11							11
12							12
13							13
14							14
15							15
16							16
17							17
18							18
19							19

3.

Name ______________________________

APPENDIX 2 PROBLEM 14-6 ___

1. and 2.

JOURNAL

PAGE

	DATE		DESCRIPTION	POST. REF.	DEBIT	CREDIT	
1							1
2							2
3							3
4							4
5							5
6							6
7							7
8							8
9							9
10							10
11							11
12							12
13							13
14							14
15							15
16							16
17							17
18							18
19							19

3.

Name ______________________________

EXERCISE 15-1

a.–d.

JOURNAL

PAGE

	DATE		DESCRIPTION	POST. REF.	DEBIT	CREDIT	
1							1
2							2
3							3
4							4
5							5
6							6
7							7
8							8
9							9
10							10
11							11
12							12
13							13
14							14
15							15
16							16
17							17
18							18
19							19
20							20
21							21
22							22

EXERCISE 15-2

a.–d.

JOURNAL PAGE

	DATE		DESCRIPTION	POST. REF.	DEBIT	CREDIT	
1							1
2							2
3							3
4							4
5							5
6							6
7							7
8							8
9							9
10							10
11							11
12							12
13							13
14							14
15							15
16							16
17							17
18							18
19							19
20							20
21							21
22							22
23							23
24							24
25							25
26							26
27							27
28							28
29							29
30							30
31							31
32							32
33							33
34							34
35							35
36							36

Name ______________________________

EXERCISE 15-3

a. and b.

JOURNAL

PAGE

DATE		DESCRIPTION	POST. REF.	DEBIT	CREDIT

EXERCISE 15-4

EXERCISE 15-5

a.–c.

JOURNAL PAGE

	DATE		DESCRIPTION	POST. REF.	DEBIT	CREDIT	
1							1
2							2
3							3
4							4
5							5
6							6
7							7
8							8
9							9
10							10
11							11
12							12
13							13
14							14
15							15

EXERCISE 15-6

JOURNAL PAGE

	DATE		DESCRIPTION	POST. REF.	DEBIT	CREDIT	
1							1
2							2
3							3
4							4
5							5
6							6
7							7
8							8
9							9
10							10
11							11
12							12
13							13
14							14
15							15

EXERCISE 15-7

JOURNAL

PAGE

	DATE		DESCRIPTION	POST. REF.	DEBIT	CREDIT	
1							1
2							2
3							3
4							4
5							5
6							6
7							7
8							8
9							9
10							10
11							11
12							12
13							13
14							14
15							15
16							16
17							17
18							18
19							19
20							20
21							21
22							22
23							23
24							24

EXERCISE 15-8

a. and b.

JOURNAL

PAGE

	DATE		DESCRIPTION	POST. REF.	DEBIT	CREDIT	
1							1
2							2
3							3
4							4
5							5
6							6
7							7

EXERCISE 15-9

a.–b.

JOURNAL PAGE

	DATE		DESCRIPTION	POST. REF.	DEBIT	CREDIT	
1							1
2							2
3							3
4							4
5							5
6							6
7							7
8							8
9							9

EXERCISE 15-10

a.

JOURNAL PAGE

	DATE		DESCRIPTION	POST. REF.	DEBIT	CREDIT	
1							1
2							2
3							3
4							4
5							5
6							6
7							7
8							8
9							9
10							10
11							11
12							12
13							13
14							14

b.

EXERCISE 15-11

EXERCISE 15-12

Lydell Capital, Inc.

Selected Income Statement Items

For the Years Ended December 31, 2010 and 2011

	2010	2011
Operating income	a. ________	e. ________
Unrealized gain (loss)	b. ________	$ (2,000)
Net income	c. ________	14,000

Lydell Capital, Inc.

Selected Balance Sheet Items

December 31, 2009, 2010, and 2011

	Dec. 31, 2009	Dec. 31, 2010	Dec. 31, 2011
Trading investments, at cost	$123,000	$146,000	$172,000
Valuation allowance for investments	(6,000)	9,000	g. ________
Trading investments, at fair value	d. ________	f. ________	h. ________
Retained earnings	$145,000	$192,000	i. ________

EXERCISE 15-13

a.

JOURNAL PAGE

	DATE		DESCRIPTION	POST. REF.	DEBIT	CREDIT	
1							1
2							2
3							3
4							4
5							5
6							6
7							7
8							8
9							9
10							10
11							11
12							12
13							13
14							14
15							15
16							16

b. ______________________

Name ____________________

EXERCISE 15-14

a.–c.

JOURNAL

PAGE

	DATE		DESCRIPTION	POST. REF.	DEBIT	CREDIT	
1							1
2							2
3							3
4							4
5							5
6							6
7							7
8							8
9							9
10							10
11							11
12							12
13							13
14							14
15							15
16							16
17							17
18							18
19							19
20							20

Computations:

EXERCISE 15-15

a. 1.

JOURNAL

PAGE

	DATE		DESCRIPTION	POST. REF.	DEBIT	CREDIT	
1							1
2							2
3							3
4							4
5							5
6							6
7							7

Computations:

a. 2.

JOURNAL

PAGE

	DATE		DESCRIPTION	POST. REF.	DEBIT	CREDIT	
1							1
2							2
3							3
4							4
5							5

Computations:

Name ______________________________

EXERCISE 15-15, Concluded

Computations:

b. ______________________________

EXERCISE 15-16

a.

b.

EXERCISE 15-17

Oceanic Airways
Selected Income Statement Items
For the Years Ended December 31, 2010 and 2011

	2010	2011
Operating income	a. ________	g. ________
Gain (loss) from sale of investments	$4,000	$ (8,000)
Net income	b. ________	(11,000)

Oceanic Airways
Selected Balance Sheet Items
December 31, 2009, 2010, and 2011

	Dec. 31, 2009	Dec. 31, 2010	Dec. 31, 2011
Assets			
Available-for-sale investments, at cost	$ 78,000	$ 68,000	$95,000
Valuation allowance for available-for-sale investments	5,000	(6,000)	h. ________
Available-for-sale investments, at fair value	c. ________	e. ________	i. ________
Stockholders' Equity			
Unrealized gain (loss) on available-for-sale investments	d. ________	f. ________	(7,000)
Retained earnings	$164,000	$232,000	j. ________

Name ______________________________

EXERCISE 15-18

a.

JOURNAL PAGE

DATE		DESCRIPTION	POST. REF.	DEBIT	CREDIT

b. ______________________________

____

____

____

____

____

____

c. ______________________________

____

____

____

EXERCISE 15-19

a.–c.

JOURNAL PAGE

DATE		DESCRIPTION	POST. REF.	DEBIT	CREDIT

Computations:

Name ______________________________

EXERCISE 15-20

a. 1.

JOURNAL PAGE

	DATE		DESCRIPTION	POST. REF.	DEBIT	CREDIT	
1							1
2							2
3							3
4							4
5							5
6							6
7							7

Computations:

a. 2.

JOURNAL PAGE

	DATE		DESCRIPTION	POST. REF.	DEBIT	CREDIT	
1							1
2							2
3							3
4							4
5							5

Computations:

EXERCISE 15-20, Concluded

Computations:

b.

EXERCISE 15-21

a.

Balance Sheet (selected items)

EXERCISE 15-21, Concluded

b.

Balance Sheet (selected items)

EXERCISE 15-22

Stockholders' Equity

APPENDIX 1 EXERCISE 15-23

a. and b.

JOURNAL PAGE

	DATE		DESCRIPTION	POST. REF.	DEBIT	CREDIT	
1							1
2							2
3							3
4							4
5							5
6							6
7							7
8							8
9							9
10							10
11							11
12							12
13							13
14							14
15							15
16							16
17							17
18							18

c. ____

Name ______________________________

APPENDIX 1 EXERCISE 15-24

a. and b.

JOURNAL PAGE

	DATE		DESCRIPTION	POST. REF.	DEBIT	CREDIT	
1							1
2							2
3							3
4							4
5							5
6							6
7							7
8							8
9							9
10							10
11							11
12							12
13							13
14							14
15							15
16							16
17							17
18							18

c. ______________________________

APPENDIX 1 EXERCISE 15-25

a.–e.

JOURNAL

PAGE

DATE		DESCRIPTION	POST. REF.	DEBIT	CREDIT

Name ____

APPENDIX 1 EXERCISE 15-26

JOURNAL

PAGE

DATE		DESCRIPTION	POST. REF.	DEBIT	CREDIT

APPENDIX 2 EXERCISE 15-27

Statement of Comprehensive Income

APPENDIX 2 EXERCISE 15-28

Statement of Comprehensive Income

Name ______________________________

EXERCISE 15-29

Dividend Yield: ______________________________

EXERCISE 15-30

a. 2006: Dividend Yield: ______________________________

2007: Dividend Yield: ______________________________

b. ______________________________

EXERCISE 15-31

PROBLEM 15-1 ___

1.

JOURNAL

PAGE

	DATE		DESCRIPTION	POST. REF.	DEBIT	CREDIT	
1	*2010*						1
2							2
3							3
4							4
5							5
6							6
7							7
8							8
9							9
10							10
11							11
12							12
13							13
14							14
15							15
16							16
17							17
18							18
19							19
20							20
21							21
22							22
23							23
24							24
25							25
26							26
27							27
28							28
29							29
30							30
31							31
32							32
33							33
34							34
35							35
36							36

PROBLEM 15-1 ___, Continued

JOURNAL

PAGE

	DATE		DESCRIPTION	POST. REF.	DEBIT	CREDIT	
1							1
2							2
3							3
4							4
5							5
6							6
7							7
8							8
9							9
10							10
11							11
12							12
13							13
14							14
15							15
16							16
17							17
18							18
19							19
20							20

Calculations:

PROBLEM 15-1 ___, Concluded

2.

Balance Sheet (selected items)

PROBLEM 15-2 ___

1. **JOURNAL** PAGE

	DATE		DESCRIPTION	POST. REF.	DEBIT	CREDIT	
1	*2010*						1
2							2
3							3
4							4
5							5
6							6
7							7
8							8
9							9
10							10
11							11
12							12
13							13
14							14
15							15
16							16
17							17
18							18
19							19
20							20
21							21
22							22
23							23

Calculations:

PROBLEM 15-2 ___, Continued

1. **JOURNAL** PAGE

	DATE		DESCRIPTION	POST. REF.	DEBIT	CREDIT	
1	*2011*						1
2							2
3							3
4							4
5							5
6							6
7							7
8							8
9							9
10							10
11							11
12							12
13							13
14							14
15							15
16							16
17							17
18							18
19							19

Calculations:

PROBLEM 15-2 ___, Concluded

2.

Balance Sheet (selected items)

3.

Name ______________________________

PROBLEM 15-3 ___

1.

JOURNAL

PAGE

	DATE		DESCRIPTION	POST. REF.	DEBIT	CREDIT	
1	*2010*						1
2							2
3							3
4							4
5							5
6							6
7							7
8							8
9							9
10							10
11							11
12							12
13							13
14							14
15							15
16							16
17							17
18							18
19							19
20							20
21							21
22							22
23							23
24							24
25							25
26							26
27							27
28							28
29							29
30							30
31							31
32							32
33							33
34							34
35							35
36							36

PROBLEM 15-3 ___, Continued

JOURNAL

PAGE

	DATE		DESCRIPTION	POST. REF.	DEBIT	CREDIT	
1	2010						1
2							2
3							3
4							4
5							5
6							6
7							7
8							8

Calculations:

PROBLEM 15-3 ___, Continued

JOURNAL

PAGE

	DATE		DESCRIPTION	POST. REF.	DEBIT	CREDIT	
1	2011						1
2							2
3							3
4							4
5							5
6							6
7							7
8							8
9							9
10							10
11							11
12							12
13							13
14							14
15							15
16							16
17							17
18							18

Calculations:

PROBLEM 15-3 ___, Concluded

2.

Balance Sheet (selected items)

Name ______________________________

PROBLEM 15-4 ___

1. a. ______________________________

   b. ______________________________

   c. ______________________________

Calculations:

d. ______________________________

e. ______________________________

f. ______________________________

g. ______________________________

h. ______________________________

i. ______________________________

PROBLEM 15-4 ___, Continued

Completed comparative unclassified balance sheet (optional):

Balance Sheet

	DEC. 31, 2011	DEC. 31, 2010

For December 31, 2010:

PROBLEM 15-4 ___, Concluded

For December 31, 2011:

Name ______________________

COMPREHENSIVE PROBLEM 4

1.

JOURNAL

PAGE

	DATE		DESCRIPTION	POST. REF.	DEBIT	CREDIT	
1							1
2							2
3							3
4							4
5							5
6							6
7							7
8							8
9							9
10							10
11							11
12							12
13							13
14							14
15							15
16							16
17							17
18							18
19							19
20							20
21							21
22							22
23							23
24							24
25							25
26							26
27							27
28							28
29							29
30							30
31							31
32							32
33							33
34							34
35							35
36							36

COMPREHENSIVE PROBLEM 4, Continued

JOURNAL

PAGE

	DATE		DESCRIPTION	POST. REF.	DEBIT	CREDIT	
1							1
2							2
3							3
4							4
5							5
6							6
7							7
8							8
9							9
10							10
11							11
12							12
13							13
14							14
15							15
16							16
17							17
18							18
19							19
20							20
21							21
22							22
23							23
24							24
25							25
26							26
27							27
28							28
29							29
30							30
31							31
32							32
33							33
34							34
35							35
36							36

Name ______________________________

COMPREHENSIVE PROBLEM 4, Continued

JOURNAL

PAGE

	DATE		DESCRIPTION	POST. REF.	DEBIT	CREDIT	
1							1
2							2
3							3
4							4
5							5
6							6
7							7
8							8
9							9
10							10
11							11
12							12
13							13
14							14
15							15
16							16
17							17
18							18
19							19
20							20
21							21
22							22
23							23
24							24
25							25
26							26
27							27
28							28
29							29
30							30
31							31
32							32
33							33
34							34
35							35
36							36

COMPREHENSIVE PROBLEM 4, Continued

2. a.

Income Statement

COMPREHENSIVE PROBLEM 4, Continued

b.

Retained Earnings Statement

COMPREHENSIVE PROBLEM 4, Continued

c.

Balance Sheet

COMPREHENSIVE PROBLEM 4, Concluded

Balance Sheet (continued)

EXERCISE 16-1

____

____

____

____

____

____

____

____

____

____

EXERCISE 16-2

a. ______________________________

b. ______________________________

c. ______________________________

d. ______________________________

e. ______________________________

f. ______________________________

g. ______________________________

h. ______________________________

EXERCISE 16-3

a. Issued common stock: ______________________________

b. Redeemed bonds: ______________________________

c. Issued preferred stock: ______________________________

d. Purchased patents: ______________________________

e. Net income: ______________________________

f. Paid cash dividends: ______________________________

g. Purchased treasury stock: ______________________________

h. Sold long-term investments: ______________________________

i. Sold equipment: ______________________________

j. Purchased buildings: ______________________________

k. Issued bonds: ______________________________

EXERCISE 16-4

a. Decrease in accounts receivable: ______________________

b. Increase in notes payable due in 90 days to vendors: ______________________

c. Decrease in salaries payable: ______________________

d. Decrease in prepaid expenses: ______________________

e. Gain on retirement of long-term debt: ______________________

f. Decrease in accounts payable: ______________________

g. Increase in notes receivable due in 90 days from customers: ______________________

h. Depreciation of fixed assets: ______________________

i. Increase in merchandise inventory: ______________________

j. Amortization of patent: ______________________

k. Loss on disposal of fixed assets: ______________________

EXERCISE 16-5

EXERCISE 16-6

a.

b. ____________________

____

____

EXERCISE 16-7

EXERCISE 16-8

EXERCISE 16-9

EXERCISE 16-10

EXERCISE 16-11

EXERCISE 16-12

EXERCISE 16-13

EXERCISE 16-14

EXERCISE 16-15

EXERCISE 16-16

a.

Cash Flows from Operating Activities

b.

EXERCISE 16-17

Statement of Cash Flows

Name ______________________________

EXERCISE 16-18

EXERCISE 16-18, Concluded
(Optional)

Statement of Cash Flows

EXERCISE 16-19

a. and b.

EXERCISE 16-20

EXERCISE 16-21

a.

b.

EXERCISE 16-22

Computations:

PROBLEM 16-1 ___

Statement of Cash Flows

PROBLEM 16-1 ___, Concluded

The use of this form is not required unless so indicated by the instructor.

	A	B	C	D	E
1					
2	Spreadsheet (Work Sheet) for Statement of Cash Flows				
3					
4					
5		Balance,	Transactions		Balance,
6		________	Debit	Credit	________
7					
8					
9					
10					
11					
12					
13					
14					
15					
16					
17					
18					
19					
20					
21					
22					
23					
24					
25					
26					
27					
28					
29					
30					
31					
32					
33					
34					
35					
36					
37					

Name ______________________________

PROBLEM 16-2 ___

Statement of Cash Flows

PROBLEM 16-2 ___, Continued

The use of this form is not required unless so indicated by the instructor.

	A	B	C	D	E
1					
2	Spreadsheet (Work Sheet) for Statement of Cash Flows				
3					
4					
5		Balance,	Transactions		Balance,
6		______	Debit	Credit	______
7					
8					
9					
10					
11					
12					
13					
14					
15					
16					
17					
18					
19					
20					
21					
22					
23					
24					
25					
26					
27					
28					
29					
30					
31					
32					

Name ________________________________

PROBLEM 16-2 ___, Concluded

The use of this form is not required unless so indicated by the instructor.

	A	B	C	D	E
1					
2	Spreadsheet (Work Sheet) for Statement of Cash Flows				
3					
4					
5		Balance,	Transactions		Balance,
6		______________	Debit	Credit	______________
7					
8					
9					
10					
11					
12					
13					
14					
15					
16					
17					
18					
19					
20					
21					
22					
23					
24					
25					

Name ____________________

PROBLEM 16-3 ___

Statement of Cash Flows

PROBLEM 16-3 ___, Concluded

The use of this form is not required unless so indicated by the instructor.

	A	B	C	D	E
1					
2	Spreadsheet (Work Sheet) for Statement of Cash Flows				
3					
4					
5		Balance,	Transactions		Balance,
6		________	Debit	Credit	________
7					
8					
9					
10					
11					
12					
13					
14					
15					
16					
17					
18					
19					
20					
21					
22					
23					
24					
25					
26					
27					
28					
29					
30					
31					
32					
33					
34					
35					
36					
37					
38					
39					
40					
41					

Name ________________________________

PROBLEM 16-4 ___

Statement of Cash Flows

PROBLEM 16-4 ___, Concluded

Statement of Cash Flows (continued)

Computations:

Name ______________________________

PROBLEM 16-5 ___

Statement of Cash Flows

PROBLEM 16-5 ___, Concluded

Statement of Cash Flows (continued)

Computations:

Name ____________________

EXERCISE 17-1

a.

Comparative Income Statement

	2010		2009	
	AMOUNT	PERCENT	AMOUNT	PERCENT

b.

EXERCISE 17-2

a.

Comparative Income Statement (in thousands of dollars)

	2006		2005	
	AMOUNT	PERCENT	AMOUNT	PERCENT

b.

Name ______________________________

EXERCISE 17-3

a.

Common-Sized Income Statement

	SORENSON ELECTRONICS COMPANY		ELECTRONICS INDUSTRY AVERAGE
	AMOUNT	PERCENT	

b.

EXERCISE 17-4

Comparative Balance Sheet

	2010		2009	
	AMOUNT	PERCENT	AMOUNT	PERCENT

EXERCISE 17-5

a.

Comparative Income Statement

	2010 AMOUNT	2009 AMOUNT	INCREASE (DECREASE)	
			AMOUNT	PERCENT

b. ____

EXERCISE 17-6

a. (1) Working Capital = ______________________________

____

2010: ______________________________

____

2009: ______________________________

____

(2) Current Ratio = ______________________________

____

2010: ______________________________

____

2009: ______________________________

____

(3) Quick Ratio = ______________________________

____

2010: ______________________________

____

2009: ______________________________

____

b. ______________________________

____

____

____

____

____

EXERCISE 17-7

a. (1) Current Ratio = ______________________________

____

Dec. 30, 2006: ______________________________

____

Dec. 31, 2005: ______________________________

____

EXERCISE 17-7, Concluded

(2) Quick Ratio =

Dec. 30, 2006:

Dec. 31, 2005:

b.

EXERCISE 17-8

a.

The correct calculations are:

Working Capital =

Current Ratio =

Quick Ratio =

EXERCISE 17-8, Concluded

b. ______________________________

EXERCISE 17-9

a. (1) Accounts Receivable Turnover = ______________________________

2010: ______________________________

2009: ______________________________

(2) Number of Days' Sales in Receivables = ______________________________

2010: ______________________________

2009: ______________________________

b. ______________________________

EXERCISE 17-10

a. (1) Accounts Receivable Turnover = ____________________

Xavier: ____________________

Lestrade: ____________________

(2) Number of Days' Sales in Receivables = ____________________

Xavier: ____________________

Lestrade: ____________________

b. ____________________

EXERCISE 17-11

a. (1) Inventory Turnover = ____________________

Current Year: ____________________

Preceding Year: ____________________

EXERCISE 17-11, Concluded

(2) Number of Days' Sales in Inventory = ____________________

____

Current Year: ____________________

____

Preceding Year: ____________________

____

____

____

b. ____________________

____

____

____

____

____

EXERCISE 17-12

a. (1) Inventory Turnover = ____________________

____

Dell: ____________________

____

HP: ____________________

____

(2) Number of Days' Sales in Inventory = ____________________

____

Dell: ____________________

____

HP: ____________________

____

____

____

EXERCISE 17-12, Concluded

b. ______________________

EXERCISE 17-13

a. Ratio of Liabilities to Stockholders' Equity = ______________________

Dec. 31, 2010: ______________________

Dec. 31, 2009: ______________________

b. Number of Times Bond Interest Charges Are Earned = ______________________

Dec. 31, 2010: ______________________

Dec. 31, 2009: ______________________

EXERCISE 17-13, Concluded

c. ______________________

EXERCISE 17-14

a. Ratio of Liabilities to Stockholders' Equity = ______________________

Hasbro: ______________________

Mattel, Inc.: ______________________

b. Number of Times Interest Charges Are Earned = ______________________

Hasbro: ______________________

Mattel, Inc.: ______________________

c. ______________________

EXERCISE 17-15

a. Ratio of Liabilities to Stockholders' Equity = ______________________

____

H. J. Heinz: ______________________

____

Hershey: ______________________

____

b. Ratio of Fixed Assets to Long-Term Liabilities = ______________________

____

H. J. Heinz: ______________________

____

Hershey: ______________________

____

c. ______________________

EXERCISE 17-16

a. Ratio of Net Sales to Total Assets = ____________________

YRC Worldwide: ____________________

Union Pacific: ____________________

C. H. Robinson Worldwide, Inc.: ____________________

b. ____________________

EXERCISE 17-17

a. Rate Earned on Total Assets = ____________________

2010: ____________________

2009: ____________________

Rate Earned on Stockholders' Equity = ____________________

2010: ____________________

2009: ____________________

Rate Earned on Common Stockholders' Equity = ____________________

2010: ____________________

2009: ____________________

b. ____________________

EXERCISE 17-18

a. Rate Earned on Total Assets = ______________________

Fiscal Year 2006: ______________________

Fiscal Year 2005: ______________________

b. Rate Earned on Stockholders' Equity = ______________________

Fiscal Year 2006: ______________________

Fiscal Year 2005: ______________________

c. ______________________

d. ______________________

EXERCISE 17-19

a. Ratio of Fixed Assets to Long-Term Liabilities = ______________________

b. Ratio of Liabilities to Stockholders' Equity = ______________________

c. Ratio of Net Sales to Assets = ______________________

d. Rate Earned on Total Assets = ______________________

e. Rate Earned on Stockholders' Equity = ______________________

f. Rate Earned on Common Stockholders' Equity = ______________________

Name ______________________________

EXERCISE 17-20

a. Number of Times Bond Interest Charges Are Earned = ______________________________

b. Number of Times Preferred Dividends Are Earned = ______________________________

c. Earnings per Share on Common Stock = ______________________________

d. Price-Earnings Ratio = ______________________________

e. Dividends per Share of Common Stock = ______________________________

f. Dividend Yield = ______________________________

EXERCISE 17-21

a. Earnings per Share = ______________________

b. Price-Earnings Ratio = ______________________

c. Dividends per Share = ______________________

d. Dividend Yield = ______________________

APPENDIX EXERCISE 17-22

a. Price-Earnings Ratio = ____________________

Bank of America: ____________________

eBay: ____________________

Coca-Cola: ____________________

Dividend Yield = ____________________

Bank of America: ____________________

eBay: ____________________

Coca-Cola: ____________________

b. ____________________

APPENDIX EXERCISE 17-23

a. Earnings per share on income before extraordinary items:

Earnings Before Extraordinary Items per Share on Common Stock = ______________________

b. Earnings per Share on Common Stock = ______________________

APPENDIX EXERCISE 17-24

a. ______________________

b. ______________________

c. ______________________

d. ______________________

e. ______________________

f. ______________________

g. ______________________

Name ____________________

APPENDIX EXERCISE 17-25

a.

Partial Income Statement

b.

Partial Income Statement

APPENDIX EXERCISE 17-26

a. ____

____

____

____

____

____

b. ____

____

____

____

____

____

Name ______________________________

PROBLEM 17-1 ___

1.

Comparative Income Statement

	2010	2009	INCREASE (DECREASE)	
			AMOUNT	PERCENT

2.

____

____

____

____

____

____

____

____

____

____

Name ______________________________

PROBLEM 17-2 ___

1.

Comparative Income Statement

	2010		2009	
	AMOUNT	PERCENT	AMOUNT	PERCENT

2.

Name ______________________________

PROBLEM 17-3 ___

1. **a.** Working Capital = ______________________________

b. Current Ratio = ______________________________

c. Quick Ratio = ______________________________

PROBLEM 17-3 ___, Concluded

2.

Transaction	Working Capital	Current Ratio	Quick Ratio
a.			
b.			
c.			
d.			
e.			
f.			
g.			
h.			
i.			
j.			

Supporting calculations:

Transaction	Current Assets	Quick Assets	Current Liabilities
a.			
b.			
c.			
d.			
e.			
f.			
g.			
h.			
i.			
j.			

Name ______________________________

PROBLEM 17-4 ___

1. through 19.

1. Working Capital: ______________________________

Ratio	Numerator	Denominator	Calculated Value
2. Current ratio			
3. Quick ratio			
4. Accounts receivable turnover			
5. Number of days' sales in receivables			
6. Inventory turnover			
7. Number of days' sales in inventory			
8. Ratio of fixed assets to long-term liabilities			
9. Ratio of liabilities to stockholders' equity			
10. Number of times interest charges earned			
11. Number of times preferred dividends earned			
12. Ratio of net sales to assets			
13. Rate earned on total assets			
14. Rate earned on stockholders' equity			
15. Rate earned on common stockholders' equity			
16. Earnings per share on common stock			

PROBLEM 17-4 ___, Concluded

Ratio	Numerator	Denominator	Calculated Value
17. Price-earnings ratio			
18. Dividends per share of common stock			
19. Dividend yield			

PROBLEM 17-5 ___

1. a.

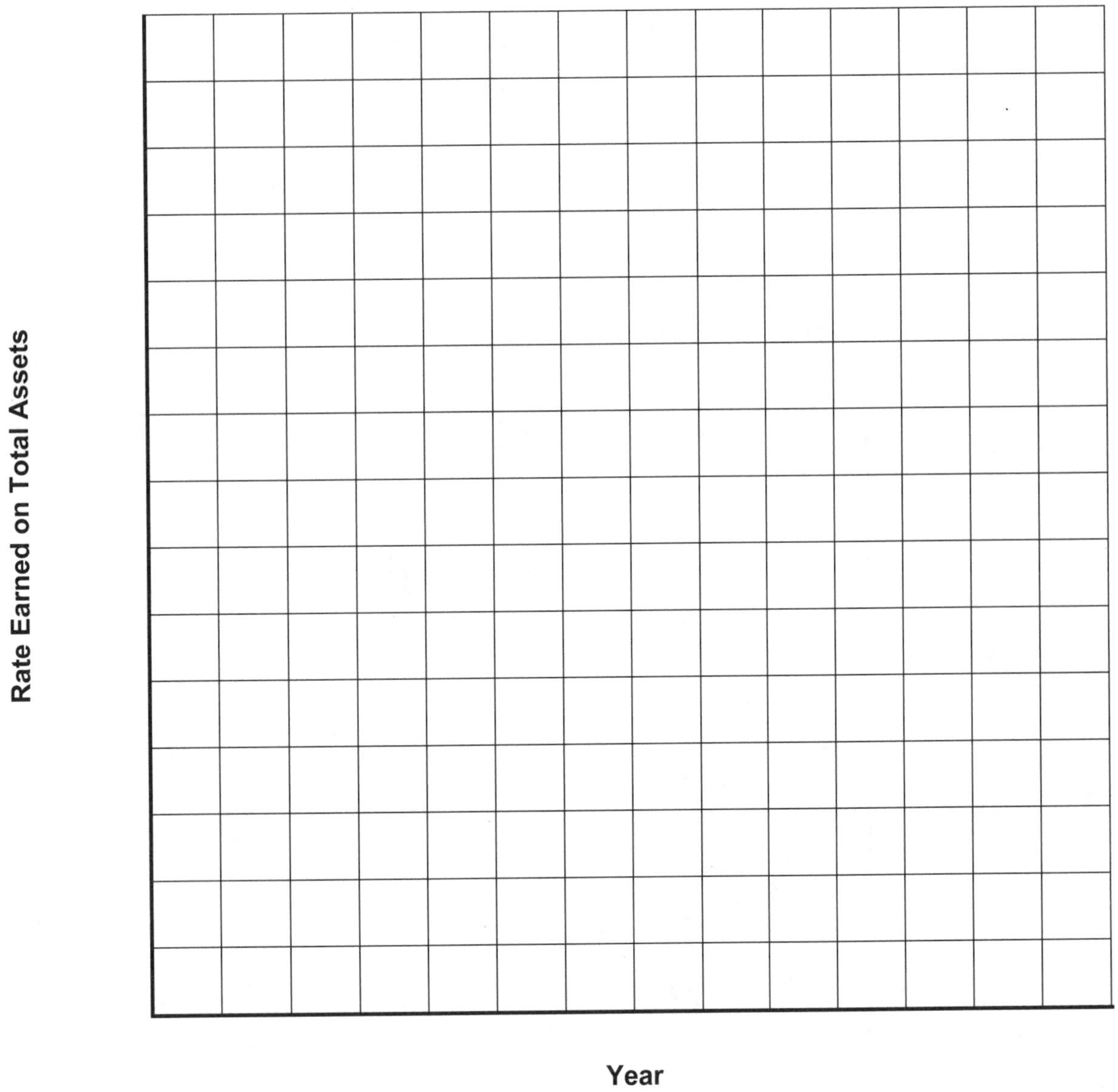

Rate Earned on Total Assets = ______________________________

____

2010: ______________ 2007: ______________

____

2009: ______________ 2006: ______________

____

2008: ______________________________

____

PROBLEM 17-5 ___, Continued

1. b.

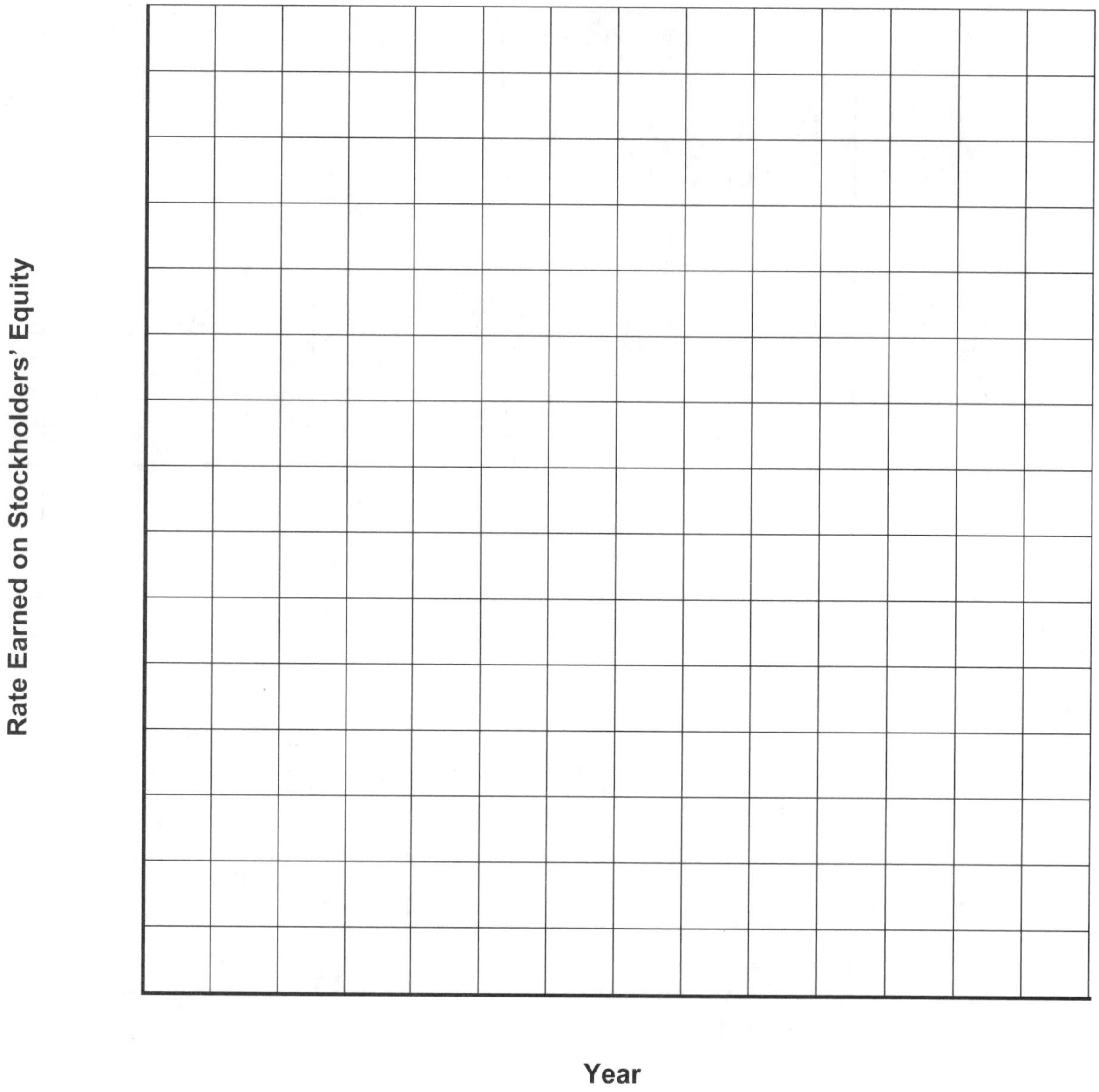

Rate Earned on Stockholders' Equity = ____________________

____

2010: ____________________ 2007: ____________________

____

2009: ____________________ 2006: ____________________

____

2008: ____________________

____

PROBLEM 17-5 ___, Continued

1. c.

Number of Times Interest Charges Earned

Year

Number of Times Interest Charges Earned = ________________________________

____

2010: ________________ 2007: ________________

____

2009: ________________ 2006: ________________

____

2008: ________________

____

PROBLEM 17-5 ___, Continued

1. d.

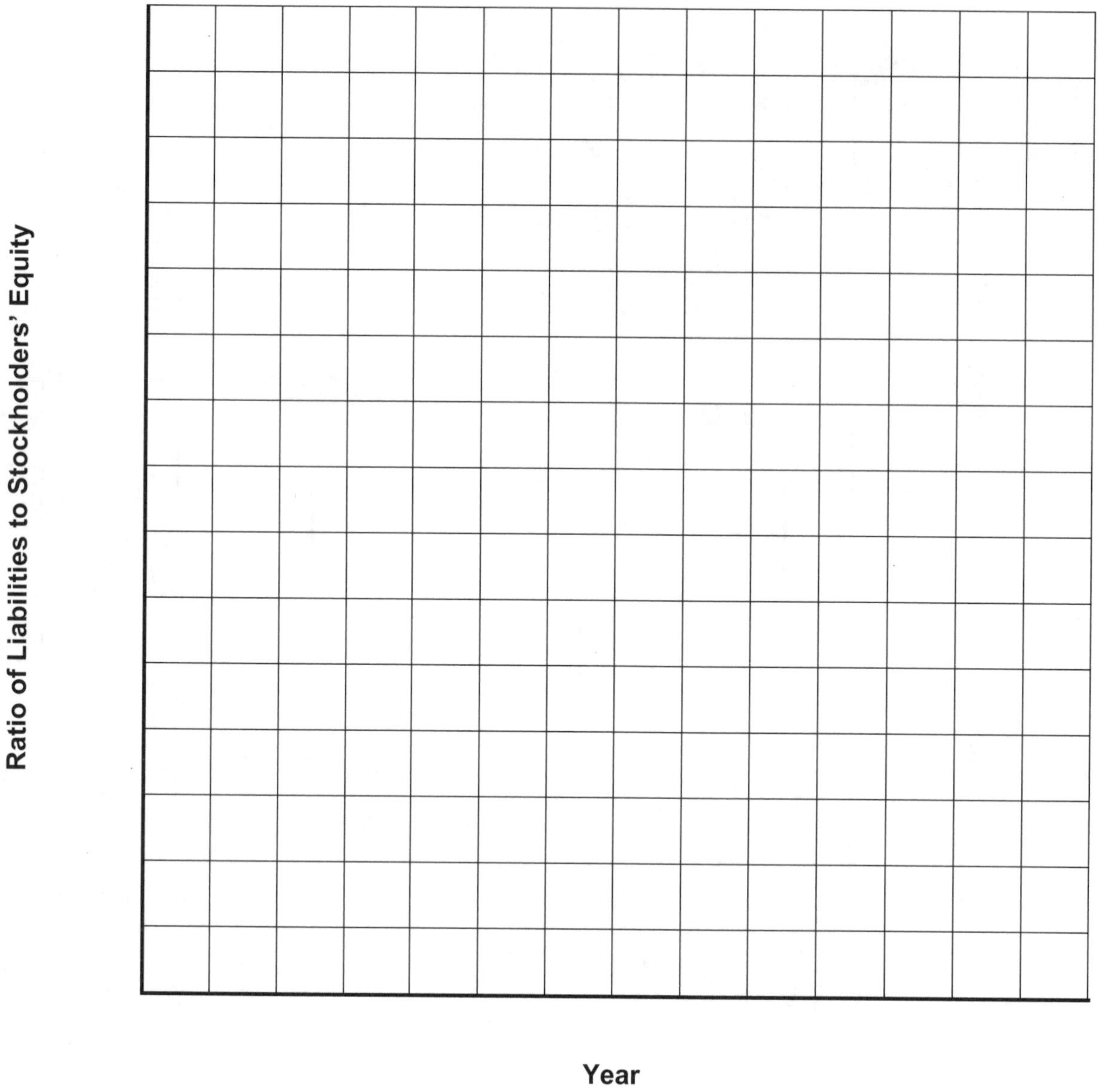

Ratio of Liabilities to Stockholders' Equity = ______________________________

____

2010: ______________ 2007: ______________

____

2009: ______________ 2006: ______________

____

2008: ______________________________

____

Name ______________________________

PROBLEM 17-5 ___, Concluded

2.

NIKE, INC., PROBLEM

1. a. through m.

	2007	2006

NIKE, INC., PROBLEM, Continued

	2007	2006

NIKE, INC., PROBLEM, Continued

2. a. through m.

NIKE, INC., PROBLEM, Concluded

Name ____________________________________

EXERCISE B-1

a.–b.

JOURNAL PAGE

	DATE		DESCRIPTION	POST. REF.	DEBIT	CREDIT	
1							1
2							2
3							3
4							4
5							5
6							6
7							7
8							8
9							9
10							10
11							11
12							12
13							13
14							14
15							15
16							16
17							17
18							18

EXERCISE B-2

a.–b.

JOURNAL PAGE

	DATE		DESCRIPTION	POST. REF.	DEBIT	CREDIT	
1							1
2							2
3							3
4							4
5							5
6							6
7							7
8							8
9							9
10							10
11							11
12							12
13							13
14							14
15							15
16							16
17							17
18							18

Name ____________________________________

EXERCISE B-3

a. (1) ______________________________

(2) ______________________________

(3) ______________________________

(4) ______________________________

(5) ______________________________

b. (1)–(5)

JOURNAL PAGE

	DATE		DESCRIPTION	POST. REF.	DEBIT	CREDIT	
1							1
2							2
3							3
4							4
5							5
6							6
7							7
8							8
9							9
10							10
11							11
12							12
13							13
14							14
15							15
16							16
17							17
18							18
19							19
20							20

EXERCISE B-4

a. (1) ______________________

(2) ______________________

(3) ______________________

(4) ______________________

(5) ______________________

b. (1)–(5)

JOURNAL PAGE

	DATE		DESCRIPTION	POST. REF.	DEBIT	CREDIT	
1							1
2							2
3							3
4							4
5							5
6							6
7							7
8							8
9							9
10							10
11							11
12							12
13							13
14							14
15							15
16							16
17							17
18							18
19							19
20							20

Name ____________________

PROBLEM C-1

1.

	A	B	C	D	E	F	G	H	I	J	K
1											
2			End-of-Period Spreadsheet (Work Sheet)								
3											
4		Unadjusted Trial				Adjusted Trial		Income		Balance	
5		Balance		Adjustments		Balance		Statement		Sheet	
6	Account Title	Dr.	Cr.	Dr.	Cr.	Dr.	Cr.	Dr.	Cr.	Dr.	Cr.
7											
8											
9											
10											
11											
12											
13											
14											
15											
16											
17											
18											
19											
20											
21											
22											
23											
24											
25											
26											
27											
28											
29											

Name ______________________________

PROBLEM C-1, Continued

	A	B	C	D	E	F	G	H	I	J	K
1											
2			End-of-Period Spreadsheet (Work Sheet)								
3			—Continued								
4		Unadjusted Trial				Adjusted Trial					
5		Balance		Adjustments		Balance		Income Statement		Balance Sheet	
6	Account Title	Dr.	Cr.	Dr.	Cr.	Dr.	Cr.	Dr.	Cr.	Dr.	Cr.
30											
31											
32											
33											
34											
35											
36											
37											
38											
39											
40											
41											
42											
43											
44											
45											
46											
47											
48											
49											
50											
51											
52											
53											
54											

PROBLEM C-1, Continued

2.

Income Statement

PROBLEM C-1, Continued

3.

Statement of Owner's Equity

Name ______________________________

PROBLEM C-1, Continued

4.

Balance Sheet

PROBLEM C-1, Continued

5. **JOURNAL** PAGE

	DATE		DESCRIPTION	POST. REF.	DEBIT	CREDIT	
1			*Adjusting Entries*				1
2							2
3							3
4							4
5							5
6							6
7							7
8							8
9							9
10							10
11							11
12							12
13							13
14							14
15							15
16							16
17							17
18							18
19							19
20							20
21							21
22							22
23							23
24							24
25							25
26							26
27							27
28							28
29							29
30							30
31							31
32							32
33							33
34							34
35							35
36							36

PROBLEM C-1, Concluded

6. **JOURNAL** PAGE

DATE		DESCRIPTION	POST. REF.	DEBIT	CREDIT
		Closing Entries			

Name ______________________

PROBLEM C-2

1.

	A	B	C	D	E	F	G	H	I	J	K
1											
2			End-of-Period Spreadsheet (Work Sheet)								
3											
4		Unadjusted Trial				Adjusted Trial		Income		Balance	
5		Balance		Adjustments		Balance		Statement		Sheet	
6	Account Title	Dr.	Cr.	Dr.	Cr.	Dr.	Cr.	Dr.	Cr.	Dr.	Cr.
7											
8											
9											
10											
11											
12											
13											
14											
15											
16											
17											
18											
19											
20											
21											
22											
23											
24											
25											
26											
27											
28											
29											

Name ______________________

PROBLEM C-2, Continued

	A	B	C	D	E	F	G	H	I	J	K
1											
2			End-of-Period Spreadsheet (Work Sheet)								
3			—Continued								
4		Unadjusted Trial				Adjusted Trial					
5		Balance		Adjustments		Balance		Income Statement		Balance Sheet	
6	Account Title	Dr.	Cr.	Dr.	Cr.	Dr.	Cr.	Dr.	Cr.	Dr.	Cr.
30											
31											
32											
33											
34											
35											
36											
37											
38											
39											
40											
41											
42											
43											
44											
45											
46											
47											
48											
49											
50											
51											
52											
53											
54											

Name ____________________

PROBLEM C-2, Continued

2.

Income Statement

PROBLEM C-2, Continued
3.

Statement of Owner's Equity

Name ______________________________

PROBLEM C-2, Continued

4.

Balance Sheet

PROBLEM C-2, Continued

5.

JOURNAL

PAGE

DATE		DESCRIPTION	POST. REF.	DEBIT	CREDIT
		Adjusting Entries			

Name ______________________________

PROBLEM C-2, Concluded

6.

JOURNAL

PAGE

DATE		DESCRIPTION	POST. REF.	DEBIT	CREDIT
		Closing Entries			

Name ______________________________

EXERCISE D-1

JOURNAL PAGE

	DATE		DESCRIPTION	POST. REF.	DEBIT	CREDIT	
1							1
2							2
3							3
4							4

Calculations:

EXERCISE D-2

JOURNAL PAGE

	DATE		DESCRIPTION	POST. REF.	DEBIT	CREDIT	
1							1
2							2
3							3
4							4

Calculations:

EXERCISE D-3

JOURNAL PAGE

	DATE		DESCRIPTION	POST. REF.	DEBIT	CREDIT	
1							1
2							2
3							3
4							4
5							5
6							6
7							7
8							8
9							9
10							10
11							11
12							12
13							13

PROBLEM D-1

1. and 2.

Year	Income Tax Deducted on Income Statement	Income Tax Payments for the Year	Deferred Income Tax Payable	
			Year's Addition (Deduction)	Year-End Balance

PROBLEM D-2

1. and 2.

Year	Income Tax Deducted on Income Statement	Income Tax Payments for the Year	Deferred Income Tax Payable	
			Year's Addition (Deduction)	Year-End Balance